Love, Lies & Lumbar Pain

Dating Misadventures of a Clueless Single Dad

George A. Smith

Ruby in the Rubble Publishing

While this is a non-fiction memoir, for privacy
reasons, some names, locations, and dates have
been changed. While I've tried my best to recall
conversations and details from years ago, I'm
old, and I forget stuff. I've tried to come close.

Photos by George A. Smith

First Edition, 2026

Contents

Contents   **3**

1. A Divorce Requires Marriage   5
2. The Ancient Tree Blooms Again   39
3. Love? Or Mango Sticky Rice?   49
4. Coffee and Chanel   65
5. Is That Ectoplasm between Your Teeth?   77
6. Craving Kim(she)   91
7. Gray Wolf Seeks Mate, Pup in the Den   107
8. Thai Me Up   115
9. Chassis Realignment   131
10. Me? Oedipus?   143
11. My Psychologist Is Paranoid   155
12. An Accountant Doesn't Add Up   187
13. I Mask to Impress   207
14. COVID Flag: She Took My Breath Away   221
15. Swiped Out   249
The Lumbar Gallery   271
Acknowledgements   287
The Author's First Misadventures   289

1. A Divorce Requires Marriage

When my first and only marriage crumbled like a stale Ritz cracker, I was sixty-two and clueless about online dating.

It seemed an unreliable way to find love. Instead of meeting someone in person, you shopped online, looked at photos you hoped were accurate, and put in your offer, hoping no one "outbid you."

Finding the right person on a dating app seemed as likely as me waking up one morning to discover I'd grown six-pack abs and could fit into my high school jeans.

The wild world of internet dating was a realm of the young.

As I sized up myself in the mirror, it wasn't a virile, juvenile Alpha staring back. It was a gray wolf with a limp and a bad back.

What about bars? Nope! When you're a man in your sixties walking into a bar alone, all it takes is stepping through the door for some people to peg you as a creep.

"What's he doing here? Looking for his daughter—or a senior's discount?"

"He must have come in the wrong door. The soup kitchen is down the block."

"Bet he's here to hit on young women."

Realistically, I was facing life without a copilot. To cope with my late life curveball, I played fun 'what if' games in my mind.

What if I formed an e-bike seniors gang? We'd talk tough, drink beer, forget what we just said, and nod off in our chairs, snoring.

Or, maybe, instead, *what if I organized a kinder, gentler type of crew? We'd drive through the neighborhood in golf carts, show up well before bedtime, and give free drugs to old people—like calcium supplements, statins, and Viagra.*

While forming my own posse seemed fun, it was more realistic to visualize myself doing whatever I wanted without compromising for anyone.

After my downsizing from divorce, why buy a new dresser when the kitchen drawers worked fine for socks, T-shirts, and underwear?

To save on electricity, why not use sunlight by day and the TV's glow to navigate at night? After all, I'd always be on the couch binging Netflix.

I'd steer my way to the bathroom with candles, or maybe a *Game of Thrones*-style tar torch.

With no wife, there was no one to complain about my binge gaming, whine about my taking the last piece of pizza, or insist I leave the bed for being gassy.

Dealing with stress through imaginary scenarios like that was nothing new to me.

When I was married and living in Europe in the '80s with my German wife, Brigitte, my "super power" drove her bonkers.

Back then, most German rental homes didn't include a built-in kitchen.

They had no cabinets, stove, sink, or fridge. The house didn't even have light fixtures, just wires hanging from the ceiling.

The Department of Defense, my employer, loaned me everything I needed for the kitchen, except a dishwasher, which was out of stock.

"We don't need one," I said to my wife. "We already have one."

"What do you mean?"

"Me," I replied.

Brigitte launched into space. It was too late for me to say I was joking, and that I wanted an "upgraded" dishwasher too.

As she raged, I went to a quiet place in my head, visualizing fluffy baby bunnies playing badminton.

While she orbited, I imagined a crazy *what-if.*

It could be worse. What if she were holding an AK-47? Naw. No biggie. She'd never figure out how to flip off the safety.

Why are you smiling?" she asked, jolting me back to reality. Thank goodness. My daydream had morphed.

7

The bunnies were now holding AK-47s.

When Brigitte paused, I jumped in to apologize for my mistimed grin.

Still, our divorce was far from a laugh fest.

My heart hurt. I ached most for the impact it had on my teenage daughter, Shannon, and early twenties son, Brandon.

Their parents' breakup left them stranded in a different culture without lifelong friends. All their life, they'd lived in Germany.

My failure reminded me of the famous fella who shared my last name, Captain Edward Smith.

He promised everyone a fun trip to the States, only to plow into an iceberg and sink. (*He was the Captain of the Titanic.*)

Just like Leonardo DiCaprio, my story started out with romance. In 1987, I arrived in Germany to work, met Brigitte, fell in love, and then married.

It took me a long time to give up my single years. I was a "late adopter," waiting until I was thirty-five to get married and procrastinating until I was forty to have my first child, Brandon.

It wasn't until I turned forty-five that I starred in a best supporting actor role in bringing baby number two, Shannon, into the world.

My then wife and I spent twenty-five years together in Europe, raising our two bilingual kids.

Then came the announcement that made us feel like grapes staring up at the vintner's incoming foot.

The Department of Defense said my serving almost three decades overseas with the GI's military broadcast network, AFN, was enough. It was time to return to the United States.

I walked into my boss's office, an Army colonel. He looked up from behind his large mahogany desk, asked me to take a seat, then looked me in the eyes.

"George," said my commander, "You've been here so long you're forgotten you're American."

"Kannst du das auf Deutsch sagen?" I asked. *Can you say it again in German?*

The look on his face, an escaped sigh, and a hand motion toward the door communicated that he thought my attempt to use humor to release tension wasn't appreciated.

The truth was, I knew it was coming. A number of my colleagues had already been given the "Army boot."

My son took it well. He was excited about leaving the gray skies and rain behind. He was in his thirteenth year at a German high school. My sapling wasn't "slow." His learning institution ran for that long.

Brandon dreamt of going to a college near a beach stocked with women likely to find his accent sexy.

My daughter attended a German junior high school. While Shannon would have rather stayed in lederhosen land, she understood leaving wasn't my choice, and supported the move.

Brigitte was the least enthusiastic.

"Well, if the rest of you want to go, I will—but I'll fly back to Europe twice a year to visit my mom."

Hold on. I thought.

It was clear who the needy one was here—me.

My body sputtered and shut down without adequate attention and affection.

Never-the-less, the family decided to collectively give relocation a try. I served as the point man, arriving in California in November 2013 to search for a place to live, while the family stayed in Germany for another six months to give my son time to graduate from German high school.

In 2014, I bought a home in Murrieta, California. It was a two-floor place on a cul-de-sac with a pool, hot tub, and waterfall.

None of the neighbors had barking dogs or little kids, and best of all, it was just a twenty-minute walk to the highly rated Murrieta Valley High School for Shannon.

With the "advance work" complete, the rest of the Smiths joined me in the States in June.

A few months after flying to California, Brandon moved out of the house and started school in Santa Barbara. He scored a beach view, blue skies, and oh, yes—an education.

In August, Shannon began tenth grade.

Brigitte, meanwhile, opened her laptop to launch a Google search for the best flights back to Frankfurt.

Every divorce requires a marriage.

We officially split in 2016, but were separated months before that. My ex missed Germany and her mom, disliked the States, and craved authentic schnitzel.

For me, splitting up after a quarter century of matrimony was like waking up to discover a lit firecracker bobbing in my Cheerios.

After the initial shock, I *still* wasn't sure if I wanted to fly solo.

I needed to find Ms. Right before the bone-on-bone in my knees scraped together to spark fire, and my eyebrows became the only hair left on my head.

My face didn't curdle milk, but I was no Ryan Reynolds. Sure, other divorced, wrinkled warriors went on to remarry, but my name wasn't Bezos.

Could I balance juggling single fatherhood, a full-time job, two kids (one at home and one at college), and a dating life?

While I had reasons to stay single, I believed in the product I was marketing: me. I was like *aged blue cheese*—not for the timid, but for the bold willing to give me a try—unforgettable!

It was Brandon and Shannon who helped lance my indecisiveness and prod me when I needed it. When I mentioned wanting to give dating a shot, they encouraged me to start swiping.

Hearing that, my guilt about taking time to date at the expense of spending less time with them evaporated.

It was settled. I would set off on a quest to find new love before my brain scrambled and I started pressing the TV remote to shut the garage door.

Liking round numbers, I set a goal of finding new love before I hit seventy.

The thought of dating in my sixties didn't make me feel young again. It conjured up memories of awkward encounters in my youth, rejections, and above all, crazy, quirky experiences.

At least, most of *those* dates were never boring.

In my twenties and thirties, *before* I got married, my dating experiences were more like an episode of *Seinfeld* than *Fifty Shades of Grey*.

Seven years before I met Brigitte, I was a single soldier, working as a twenty-six-year-old Army DJ in Nuremberg.

One night in 1980, I strolled into a restaurant in the shadow of the city's castle and beheld a blonde goddess who'd inexplicably descended to earth to serve mere mortals mugs of beer and plates of meat.

Or maybe she was the siren Lorelei, taking a break from singing on her favorite rock above the Rhine?

Her name was Frieda.

After a meal of Nuremberg bratwurst, potato salad, and beer, I mustered the courage to ask her out.

"Ich habe etwas viel besseres als Trinkgeld. Darf ich dich zum Abendessen einladen?" (I have something much better than a tip. May I take you to dinner?)

She said yes—officially launching a one-year romance.

One night, as we lay in bed at my apartment talking, I shared something that I'd been considering for weeks.

"I'm thinking about leaving the Army and going to college in the States."

She took a deep drag on her cigarette and exhaled slowly. Glancing over at her, I could see her face briefly glow red from the ember.

"You should do it," said Frieda. "Then come back to me."

I expected an argument, or tears. Instead, she gave me understanding and support.

After making the leap out of the service to attend Ohio University in 1981, I invited Frieda over to the States to visit me on winter break. *That's* when our relationship began to unravel.

I was a broke student with no car, so we stayed at my Mom and Dad's farm in rural Pennsylvania. Since we weren't married, my parents insisted we stay in separate rooms.

We honored that until midnight. That's when I'd sneak over to my girlfriend's room feeling more like a "hide my pimples with flesh-colored Clearasil" teenager than a man pushing thirty.

My parents had another major issue with Frieda—her smoking.

While Frieda's kisses sometimes reminded me of smoked salmon, I overlooked it.

My Dad, on the other hand, despaired that I'd brought a two-legged carbon-dioxide generator into the house.

When I complained that she had to walk outside in the cold to smoke, Dad half smiled and said, "Maybe if she does that enough, she'll quit!"

Once, in my brother David's car, Frieda fished out a cigarette and was about to light one up when she opened his ash tray and noticed it was filled with quarters, nickels, and dimes.

"What's this?"

"It's a coin tray, Frieda."

David eventually pulled the car over to give her a smoke break.

All of this started to wear on my girlfriend. To bring up her spirits and mine, I borrowed my Mom's car to take her out for some one-on-one time, but that flamed out as well.

Taking her to an American all-you-can-eat buffet was a huge mistake.

"George, these people need to spend time lifting weights, not plates of fried chicken."

Then, in a loud voice, she proceeded to turn and point out individuals who failed her height and weight standards.

I turned the color of my plate of strawberries.

"Why do you care?" I whispered. Then joked, "They can't eat it all. They'll leave some for us!"

"But, George—" she said, turning to eye a man moving past us with two plates of food stacked high like matching volcanos.

Switching into German, I got direct.

"Frieda, bitte hör auf! Das ist unhöflich! Sie können dich hören." *I told her to stop, because it was rude and they could hear her.*

Later that night, I took her to the only night club in the small town—only to fail again.

Shortly after I ordered two glasses of champagne, the waiter came over, put our drinks in front of us and sheepishly apologized for the refrigerator going out. They mostly sold beer on tap, not bubbly.

His solution? Ice cubes in our champagne. We both shook our heads and laughed.

"We're not in Germany anymore!" I said.

In a way, that botched attempt to "save" the champagne symbolized what happened to our relationship. Smoky Lips went back to Germany and I went back to Ohio University.

We parted ways, but stayed in touch as friends.

About four years later, after I graduated from college, I ventured into the world of online dating's "grandpaw"—the classified ads.

I was working in Washington, D.C. at the time when I channeled Nora Roberts and mailed a masterpiece to the *Washingtonian*.

Back then, they didn't post pictures or phone numbers. The publication served as a matchmaker, notifying posters when someone responded to their ad.

Striving for something that showcased my witty personality, I avoided the cliched "man with a sense of humor seeks same. To me, saying you have a sense of humor is just your opinion.

What counts is what other people think. I thought the best way to attract someone who liked to laugh was to make a joke. Only people who got it would respond. Oh how wrong I was!

This is what I wrote:

Average build, college-educated SWM (Single White Male) seeks slim SF (single female) between 21 and 35. I like to cook, read, and walk. I look like Brad Pitt if you have poor eyesight and it's a very foggy day.

It worked! Sherri said she wanted to meet outside a restaurant in the DuPont Circle area of Washington, D.C. She was my age, thirty-one. I served in the Army in Korea, Thailand, and Germany. She was previously with the Air Force, stationed in Japan.

We met on a Saturday afternoon in September under blue skies and temperatures in the mid-seventies. It seemed karma smiled my way.

Caught up in my thoughts, I strolled across a street on the zebra stripes without looking left or right. A car screeched to a stop. The driver waved for me to pass.

Awesome. I thought. *No pounding on the horn or rolling down the window to yell at me for almost splattering against his bumper.*

When I arrived at our rendezvous point, a woman looked my way. She struck me as a young Meg Ryan—but prettier—with neat blonde hair, blue eyes, and a svelte figure.

"George??" she asked.

"Sherri?"

"I should have asked for a photo."

"Huh?"

"You don't look like Brad Pitt."

"Uh. It's a joke," I said to her back as she hustled away.

Raising my voice so it would reach her retreating ears, I added, "It means I look like him ONLY if you have bad eyes and it's a foggy day."

Her response was the rapid clicking of her heels, as she put more space between us. I was humiliated. My blind date lasted two minutes.

A metallic *cling, cling* accompanied by a loud "move" jolted me out of my self-pity and shock. Turning, I glimpsed a bike rider swerving around me, clicking away on his bell with his thumb.

I was wrong. Karma wasn't smiling. He was laughing at me.

Walking back to my car, I replayed the brief exchange through Sherri's eyes. To her, I was lying about my looks to trick her into a date.

Ouch.

My next rendezvous came with a 5-foot-6 blonde who understood my self-deprecating jokes. It started well, but ended in a bizarre twist.

Pam and I met at the Chart House restaurant in Old Town Alexandria along the Potomac River.

We laughed over crab cakes and sea bass when I shared my sad tale of meeting a woman who took one look at me, disapproved, and left me standing with my jaw dangling.

"Well, it sounds like you dodged a shallow one with no sense of humor," said my date, who later revealed she was an insurance agent.

The night held promise. She asked if I wanted to go to her place. Flattered, I paused for a few seconds so I wouldn't sound easy.

"Sure."

I followed her to a mobile home on the edge of town. When she opened the door, stale air escaped.

Pam flipped on a light as my eyes adjusted.

She must have lubed the furniture with Crisco to get it to fit. My date somehow squeezed a couch, TV, kitchen table and chairs, and an eight-foot-long raised hard plastic surface with the outline of a man on it into her small mobile home.

The wall art? Cross sections of humans: skin, muscles, and internal organs. The sides of the "person" counter had levers and switches mounted on a metal pedestal.

All that was missing was Dr. Frankenstein and bolts of lightning. Was her real name Igora?

"What's that?" I asked, simultaneously backpedaling for the door.

"That's my spa table," Pam said. "I have two jobs."

Before I responded, she continued, "But I don't give massages to dates. That's for clients."

"Dates" as in the plural?

Hmmm, I thought. *How many have been here, and how many would follow me? And where was the sign out front advertising "rubdown studio?"*

"Let's sit down and relax," she said, flicking her thumb in the direction of the couch. "Beer?"

"Sure," I answered, as she turned the TV on and flipped to a *Star Trek* rerun. The theme song and Kirk's words, "To boldly go where no man has gone before" mixed with the faint chirping of crickets outside the mobile home.

Flushed with excitement, I hoped whatever she suggested next didn't include the two of us sprawled on the plastic table with an outline of a man—a weird threesome.

The "work surface" wasn't the only item in the trailer radiating strangeness. While attracted to her, the cramped, forced atmosphere with human anatomy "art" churned my belly.

Part of my angst stemmed from binging science fiction. Scenes from *Soylent Green, The Walking Dead,* and *Repo Men* looped in my mind.

Testosterone prevailed over paranoia. I slid my hand around her shoulder, then stopped, noting tears slipping from her eyes.

Wow, I thought. *I've never seen anyone so touched by Captain Kirk's dialogue.*

"What's up?"

She dialed down the TV volume, then swiveled to look me in the eyes to assure me it was nothing.

Then, unexplainably, the outside cricket chorus stopped. The stale air turned musky. As I squinted into the dark corner of the room, a pair of greenish-yellow eyes came into focus.

Aaaaachu, sprayed Pam.

"What the hell is that?" I blurted, standing up and pointing at the orbs staring out from behind a wooden children's gate.

"Oh! (sneeze, dribble, sniff). *That's* Tinkerbell."

On cue, a beast with a pink collar moved out of the shadows.

"You didn't mention you have a pooch the size of a pony."

"Well," she said. "I worried you'd think it's weird that I have a Rottweiler in a trailer, especially since I'm allergic to dogs."

You think???

Tinkerbell's eyes locked onto me like *Star Trek* tractor beams. Saliva spotted the corners of her mouth. She remained silent.

Yum, Delivery service. I'll start with a leg, I imagined it thinking.

21

My libido melted under the gaze of the laser-eyed beast with the drool-covered teeth. I calmed myself, waited a few minutes, and looked at my watch.

Standing up, I said it was late and I had to go. Backing to the door with one eye on the hound, guilt crept in. After getting empathy from Pam on my crash and burn story of Sherri walking off right after seeing me, here I was disentangling from her on our first date.

The tributary from her eyes and the one from her nose joined together as one stream as she composed herself enough to speak.

"I hope to (sniff) see you again."

"I'll call," I said, shaking her hand and hurrying out to my car.

The next day I did—leaving a voicemail.

"Nice meeting you. But I found out I'm going on night shifts (a true statement). I'm going to have to put my dating life on hold."

As I hung up, my face flushed. I lacked the guts to tell her to her face that we weren't a good match.

In the future, I promised myself I'd "George Up," and say in person if the relationship wasn't working.

The opportunity came sooner than I expected.

The next month, Maria and I clicked on our first date to a steakhouse in Arlington. The woman, who stood 5-foot-5, with shoulder-length straight black hair, and large brown eyes, laughed about the tongue-in-cheek humor in my ad.

What's remarkable was that she got the joke even though English wasn't her first language. She was Filipino.

We sped through the mandatory first-date small talk before the conversation turned to the Philippines, which I visited when I was stationed in Thailand with the Army.

I visited Manila, the fortress of Corregidor, and Pagsanjan Falls.

"You've been to my country. I love it," she said, as we finished our filet mignons and a surprisingly tasty carafe of dry, house red wine.

We parted with smiles. Outside, right before we got into our cars to head out, I suggested I pick her up at her house for our next date.

Maria paused for a second—her face flashing a trace of doubt or concern. I couldn't quite peg it. But she recovered, smiled, and said "yes."

That weekend, as I pulled up in front of her house on the outskirts of Alexandria, I heard a din of unbridled chaos through my closed car windows. It sounded like a pack of squirrels had broken into her Monster energy drinks and Snickers bars.

Maybe it was the wrong address? But when I double-checked, it was Maria's.

When I rang the bell, I heard laughter, and my date's voice, "Keep it down, he's here."

After a few seconds, the chorus of voices quieted, and I heard the click, click of heels getting closer as my date opened the door.

"Hi, George."

During our steak dinner, she mentioned she was divorced, but kids didn't come up.

"You have kids?"

"I do. You're all okay with that, right?"

My brain spun like one of those cotton candy-making machines at the fair. I was a single guy with no children. Now I was being asked what I thought about bundles of energy residing on the other side of that door.

"Um," I stammered. "How many do you have?"

"Seven."

My lips lost the ability to form words. My mouth dried.

"Suh . . . suh . . . seven?"

Then, in a burst of clarity, I remembered my cowardly retreat from Pam and Tinkerbell the Rottweiler's home. I manned up.

"Maria, I loved our first date. It was really easy to talk with you. But I can't be the dad for seven kids. This won't work. I'm sorry."

Turning, I walked back to my car, and plopped down and felt like a pile of pig poop. Still, I had leveled with her on the spot, rather than coming up with an excuse later.

It would be my last date generated from that classified ad.

Months later, in 1985, I asked out a colleague of mine from the Voice of America, an Austrian woman, Bettina.

The blonde, full-figured beauty with flawless skin and huge blue eyes routinely made everyone on the late-night news desk pause their fingers above their keyboards in stunned admiration when she walked in.

I made a good first impression on her when I strolled over and launched into a full conversation in German. I'd picked the language up in the early '80s when I was a military DJ in Nuremberg.

My idea for our first date? I would come over to her house and make her blackened red snapper. It was a recipe I'd perfected from a book written by Louisiana Cajun Chef Paul Prudhomme.

"Are you sure you want to do that?" asked Bettina. "We could just go out to dinner."

Focused on impressing her with my culinary skills, I insisted.

Late that afternoon, I showed up with fish, butter, seasoning, and a pan to work my magic.

"Are you sure you don't want me to help?" Bettina asked.

"No," I want you to relax, I said. "I'll call you when it's ready."

"All right," she said. "But please make sure to use the stove fan."

She went upstairs as I started my culinary masterpiece in her kitchen, which, like the rest of the interior of her house, sparkled. The gas stove and white tile backsplash looked like it was staged by a real estate agent.

Then, as I blackened the fish, disaster struck.

When I turned on the overhead exhaust fan, the extra air caused the butter to catch fire. All I could see in the pan were six-inch tongues of flame.

The fish looked like it was broiling in the pits of hell.

Panicking, I searched through the kitchen for a lid to put on the pan, or something, anything, to douse the inferno.

To this day, I can't recall how I did it. I extinguished the fire, but not before splashing hot butter and burnt brown spices all over the backsplash and stove.

Then the smoke alarm went off.

Bettina came hurrying down the stairs, told me to move back, and have a seat. She cleaned up my mess in ten minutes and turned off the smoke alarm.

We had leftover potato salad that evening. It was no surprise that when I asked her for a second chance date at work the following night, the answer was a firm "nein!"

A month later, I had better luck at an Arlington, Virginia, nightclub. I met someone the old-fashioned way. I walked up and asked her to dance.

She mesmerized me with her long, straight black hair swaying to the beat of Prince's "When Doves Cry."

Her name was Rita. Her mane ran to the middle of her back. She was dancing with a girlfriend.

Stepping onto the floor, I found the experience refreshingly more direct than writing to a magazine to meet a stranger—we attracted each other.

That night sparked an intense one-year romance.

Rita introduced me to raw fish and rice wrapped in seaweed, served with soy sauce and ginger. She worked as a waitress at a top-end sushi restaurant.

Months into my relationship, my friend Jeff came to visit my high-rise apartment in Arlington to ask how Rita and I were doing. We both had donned swimsuits, lounging by the property's large swimming pool.

"So, how's the love life?" he asked.

"Hey, it looks like someone dropped a penny," I said, edging toward the water to purposely angle my back his way.

"Damn, George. Your back's covered with scratches."

"Oh. That? Yesterday I went picking raspberries, shirtless."

Turning, I looked at Jeff and smiled.

He grinned. "Good for you."

Weeks later, two friends of mine visited from Germany, staying at my apartment while seeing Washington, D.C.

Since I worked nights at Voice of America, Rita volunteered to take a day off and show them around.

They regretted taking her up on it.

"She's crazy!" said Hans-Juergen.

"I know," I said. "But could you be more specific?"

"She drives fast, doesn't look where she's going, and struggles to look over the steering wheel."

"What?"

"George, it's so bad she sits on a stack of books. Sometimes when she rounds a corner, a novel slides out, she says 'whoops,' laughs, and reaches over to pull *Tale of Two Cities* back under her butt."

Rita had just bought the car a week before my friends showed up, and I'd never been in it with her. I always took my own car into D.C. while working nights.

That night, when my two friends were asleep, I talked with my girlfriend.

"Baby, is it true you drive sitting on novels?"

"Yeah. I can't see over the wheel."

We left my apartment and went outside to the parking lot to check out her Toyota.

There in the front seat were the widest, thickest books Rita could find, stacked in layers. *The Yellow Pages* were at the bottom, with other books climbing higher like stones in a pyramid.

The first, *Tale of Two Cities*, wasn't wide enough, so it was butted next to one of my other novels, Robert Heinlein's *Stranger in a Strange Land*.

In an instant, I saw the issue. The adjustable steering wheel was at the highest elevation.

Reaching underneath the column, I flipped a lever, lowered it, and clicked it back into lock position.

Pushing her makeshift "book booster seat" to the passenger side, Rita slid in, sat down, and smiled.

"I can see!" she said, bubbling with enthusiasm as if I were some kind of master mechanic.

"Baby, please next time tell me when you're having troubles. I'll help."

"I didn't want to bother you. You're working nights, and your buddies are here."

Assuring her I would always find time to help, I asked her why my friends would say she was swerving a lot, even when sitting on top of the reading material.

"That might be because I don't wear my glasses."

"What?" I asked. "Why not?"

"I look better without them."

"Sweetie," I said, appealing to her vanity. "You'll look worse if you get in an accident and get your face cut, scratched, and scarred."

Grudgingly, she said she would don the eyewear in the future.

It became clear to me why Rita had two accidents in the eighteen months before I met her.

After my friends left, my sweetheart and I enjoyed each other's company. We even took a three-hour car ride north to visit my mom and dad's farm in Pennsylvania.

Yes, there were hiccups. Like the time she found a coupon I'd torn out of the *Washingtonian* for $2 margaritas at an Alexandria bar.

"What's this?" she asked.

"Cheap drinks. We should go!"

"No. Flip it over. The other side is advertising Rita's Ribs. You're stealing my name. You, and the CIA!"

"What?"

"You said you work for the federal government."

"Yes."

"And Voice of America falls under the CIA?"

"No, no, no. The USIA. The United States Information Agency. It's under the State Department."

I started wondering if a sushi tapeworm had nibbled away the reasoning part of her brain.

"Baby, there's more than one Rita in the world, and besides that, I don't think the CIA needs a rib joint to launder money for operations."

"Well, it just seems like a strange coincidence."

That awkward, accusatory exchange replayed in my mind later, when I was weighing whether to take an unexpected opportunity.

Uncle Sugar offered me a job running a radio/TV affiliate as a federal government employee for the Army in Nuremberg, Germany.

It didn't take me long to decide. I accepted it and decided to break the news to Rita the next day.

"But you just bought a condo and we just moved in," she said.

"I know," I told her, "It's been a year since I applied for this job, and I didn't think they wanted me, until now."

While I cared for her, and the timing sucked, the job offer forced me to confront the depth of my feelings.

The biggest difference was that I wanted kids of my own, and she physically couldn't have kids. Rita wasn't the woman I wanted to spend the rest of my life with. The relationship ended, but she continued to rent my condo for ten years.

That 1986 date with Rita was my last in the States.

Fast-forward to 2016. After my divorce, I was more than rusty. I was 180 pounds of iron oxide.

Three decades had passed since my last Stateside dating experience. Classified ads had long since stopped being a way to meet someone, unless you tried CraigsList, but I wasn't interested in love for rent or getting mugged.

Friends suggested I retire my caveman ways, walk over to the light of my computer screen, and sign up for online dating.

But you just can't point a Cro-Magnon man at a dating app and say, "Have at it!"

After living almost thirty years in Germany, I knew as much about dating apps as Kim Kardashian knew about quantum physics.

I needed help. A guide. A guru. A sensei to navigate me away from gold diggers and scammers.

My choice was Tom, a co-worker and fellow vet. His credentials? He met his wife on Zoosk.

We rendezvoused at Denny's for a complimentary Veterans Day breakfast. On the menu? The vocabulary, customs, and land mines of seeking and meeting a stranger for love.

My goal was to meet single women without mistakenly walking down a dark alley with a gorgeous woman who was secretly part of a ring harvesting kidneys for the black market.

As Tom and I chatted, he opened Tinder and told me to "swipe right." Thinking I overlooked a few specks of egg, I dabbed my napkin at my face.

"No, George," he sighed. "You move your finger right on your smartphone when you see a profile you're interested in."

I was as clueless as an out-of-towner walking down a dark alley at one a.m. to ask some meth heads if they could break a hundred.

"You're going to be the most popular guy on the internet for all the wrong reasons," my friend said.

"You're old, naive, and trusting. My sister knows more about the singles scene in California—and she's a nun."

I frowned as the scent of burnt toast and sizzling sausage mingled with the overpowering perfume of three blue-haired ladies sitting in the next booth.

They were positioned opposite a trio of men sporting "Vietnam Veteran" hats. The guys were getting animated about politics and critical about their rubbery eggs.

"Want the rest of your bacon?" I asked my pal, turning to smile as a hot Latina woman swung by our table to pour us decaf.

"She doesn't need a third grandpa in her life," laughed Tom. "Stick with a woman your age."

His dig pulled me back from the alternate universe I was frolicking in, where beautiful women saw me not as a relic, but as a salt-and-pepper-haired Adonis.

I had a sizable vocabulary. But dating required a new language. Until he explained them, the words Tom threw at me made as much sense as ancient Sumerian.

Breadcrumbing was stringing you along, peacocking was showing off, and micro-cheating was cheating a little bit.

"Cheating a little bit?" I asked. "What's that? A woman saying that it was no big deal having an open-mouthed kiss with another dude because it *only* lasted for five seconds?"

When he mentioned "pansexual," my overactive libido imagined it was a kinky woman who liked getting whacked on the butt with a skillet.

When he told me about "ghosting," I thought he was confusing dating with one of those TV shows where a camera crew sneaks into a haunted house searching for ectoplasm and blinking ceiling lights.

"Tom, no one's coming back from the dead to haunt me. They know I'd take one look, say 'cool,' and flash a thumbs up."

My friend shook his head in disbelief.

"You are certified clueless!"

Tom's face flashed frustration as I continued to struggle with the lingo.

"I'm guessing a green flag means no issues and red means avoid someone, but what about beige?"

Tom's answer?

"They've looked at your profile and think you're boring."

My pal overwhelmed me with more vocabulary over a fourth cup of joe. Of all the advice he gave, his warnings about catfishing stuck.

"Shelve your trust. If a woman says she wants to split costs to fly with you to Tahiti, but she misplaced her Visa, don't pass her your number."

"I wouldn't make that mistake," I said.

"Well, you might if you look at her picture, and she's hot. Don't bite. Chances are she's some bald, chubby guy in Pennsylvania out to trick you out of cash with some gift card scheme, or harvest your Visa number. It's catfishing."

Tap, Tap.

Turning and looking, I hoped the person tapping my shoulder was the gorgeous waitress. No luck.

The interrupting finger remained poised in the air. It belonged to one of the vets sitting in the booth next to ours.

"Are you guys Army?"

"Yup," I said. "I spent eight years in the service as a radio/TV journalist. I finished up serving thirty-five more years with the Department of Defense as a civilian."

Gesturing to my buddy, I added, "Tom served as a soldier in Japan. Now both of us work at the American Forces Network Broadcast Center here in Riverside."

The man with the U.S. flag hat pushed aside a plate with a French Toast crust slathered in syrup before responding. His hat identified him as "Chuck."

"I overheard you two jawing about apps. Don't mess with that. I have a divorced sister. You'd make a great couple."

Chuck stroked his stubble with one hand, using the other to scroll through his phone searching for photos of her. He continued talking her up.

"I mean it. She's beautiful."

"Yeah," chimed in the guy sitting next to him. "She *was* five years and three kids ago."

Chuck gave his friend a stare—trying to recover, then said, "Yeah, but once she finds the right man, she'll clean up nicely."

I wanted to ask if that meant his sis didn't plan to shower until she met Mr. Right—but then Chuck stopped scrolling and passed his cell phone to me. Looking at his sister's photo, I told him what he wanted to hear.

"She's pretty."

The third vet at his table started to speak up when Chuck cut him off.

"I'm having a conversation here," said Chuck, once again losing control of the narrative.

"Thanks," I said. "I appreciate you jumping in to give me a solid, but I'm going to stick with my plan of finding someone online."

Tom and I smiled, thanked the vets for their service, and made our way to our cars. I told my buddy I appreciated his "Dating App 101 class," shook his hand, and took off. As we walked, I took one more glance at the hot Latina waitress. Now that I was no longer a customer, she seemed to avoid looking my way.

Over the next few days I thought over the path I'd chosen. As a former DJ, I figured I needed a soundtrack to motivate me on my quest.

Feeling a bit melancholy, I selected "All by Myself" by Eric Carmen.

Then I expanded on what I learned with Tom by binging on YouTube videos and online articles.

Look out, single women! An ancient tree is ready to bloom again.

I may be old, but—hold on. I was going to say something witty, but I forgot.

2. The Ancient Tree Blooms Again

The aroma of browning banana pancakes and brewing coffee mingled one Saturday morning in Murrieta, California.

It was March 2016. I had prepared a father-daughter breakfast.

"Looks good," said Shannon, entering the kitchen and glancing at the table.

"What's in the box?"

"Tried these at a luncheon at work yesterday. I grabbed a few and took them home. They're great. Bran Muffins."

"Wow, Dad. Pancakes weren't enough? Double carbs and calories. Didn't you say that you wanted to slim down for dating?"

Cocking my hand, I almost winged a muffin at her, but didn't. Old people need their fiber.

As we sat down, I passed the cinnamon her way for the pancakes. Digging in, I shared Tom's dating tips.

"Well," she said in between bites, "Whatever you do, I hope you don't wear those black leather PX (a military department store) shoes."

"Why not? They go with all my clothes *and* my belt. After I replaced the soles and heels last month, they don't look like three-year-old shoes!"

That's all she needed to hear.

That afternoon, Shannon and I drove to the Temecula mall, and she picked out some casual footwear for me. They were made of gray fabric. To me, they looked like something a step above sneakers, but with no logo.

Later, my daughter snapped a picture of me hiking for my profile.

A few days after that, a professional photographer friend of mine shot me posing by my pool wearing casual clothes and a full-length photo of me at work wearing a tie.

After writing, then rewriting my sales pitch, I mean bio, I brought everything into work to run by some colleagues, Kate and Jef (we called him one "f" Jef) at lunch.

The three of us sat down on benches by a cement table. It was one of five situated on a porch outside our main building with an overhang to protect diners from the Southern California sun.

We caught a faint whiff of cigarette smoke from people clustered around the smoking gazebo, some fifty feet away.

Two ravens perched on a trash can between us and the puffers. They stared, willing us to drop some food.

"Forget the shots of you wearing sunglasses," said Kate. "Women want to check out what you look like. Shades hide flaws."

"Flaws?" I asked. "I'm a da Vinci!"

"More like a Rubens," laughed Jef. "Lay off the burgers! Focus on figuring out a way to showcase your sense of humor."

"How about a profile picture of me wearing my fake abs T-shirt?'

A chunk of carrot plunked me on the head, launched by Kate, who'd been munching on a mixed salad.

"George, you are going to be single for a loooong time."

"I'll dial it back," I said. "Years ago, I made a joke about myself in a classified ad and it backfired."

Jef said he understood my date's disappointment.

He advised honesty, saying that if a woman showed up and discovered my photos didn't accurately reflect the way I looked, the trust would be gone, and so would she.

Nodding my head, I finished up my microwaved chicken tandoori and garlic naan. We went back inside to finish work.

As I glanced back, the ravens hopped under our now vacant table. One of them stabbed at the carrot on the patio, then ignored it, staring at me as if to ask, *What, no meat?*

While driving home from work, I thought hard about why I was throwing myself into dating in my sixties. Sex? Well, if someone wanted my body for pleasure, it would be rude to say no, right?

But no, my hormones weren't driving me. I had already had my share of healthy physical relationships in my twenties.

I always seemed to repeat the same pattern. When I broke up with someone, I focused on the positive aspects of it. A single life gave me more time to do what I wanted.

I took solo vacations, binged TV, bar-hopped with friends, and sat in the living room reading and sipping cabernet.

Driving home, I found myself feeling the same way after my divorce when a "younger George" relationship ended. Euphoria over the momentary self-indulgence faded as loneliness crept in, and stuck.

In my sixties, the reasons for me trying online dating were more complex. My kids would soon be out on their own, and I didn't want to grow old(er) by myself.

Another part of me wanted to prove that women still found me interesting and attractive.

What complicated my search was my refusal to settle for just anyone.

I craved the company of someone who shared my love of travel, wanted to snuggle, and understood and supported the need for each of us to sometimes peel off and recharge individually.

As I pulled into the garage, I resolved to push forward.

Walking inside, I plopped down at my computer in the ground-floor office and uploaded pictures to my profile. The house was quiet.

Shannon was spending the evening at a girlfriend's house. In the midst of sending my "here I am healthy and hiking shot," a muffled sound from upstairs startled me.

Damn. I thought. *The rats are back.*

Micky's ugly cousins loved climbing a palm tree in my yard so they could scurry onto the roof and enter the attic. As a single dad on a budget, there was no way I accepted extra mouths to feed.

I believed the six-foot by three-foot strip of smooth sheet metal I wrapped around the trunk had put a stop to the unwelcome squatters. It seemed not.

"Hi, George."

My body launched into a six-inch vertical leap from a seated position. I yelled as I entered orbit over my desk.

All semblance of coherent words ceased as my eyes strained to focus.

Glancing over my shoulder lurked my ex-wife.

"Didn't mean to scare you. I stopped off to pack up some stuff."

Brigitte and I had parted on good terms. She still had a house key.

But until my adrenaline surge, I didn't know she was there.

A friend of hers had dropped her off at my place.

"What are you working on?"

"Uh, I uploaded my profile pictures and bio."

"Let's see who is out there. I'm curious."

Are you insane? Say no! It was my inner voice saying the words my lips couldn't.

The divorce was too fresh. It felt like my wife wanted to watch me cheat.

I sat there paralyzed.

Brigitte mistook my shocked silence as approving her as co-navigator.

"Come on. I want to help," she said, grabbing my clicker and scrolling through profiles.

"Hold on," I said, surrendering, but taking back control of my mouse. "I'll show you a few I'm considering."

The encounter was surreal. While she was no longer my wife, my face turned the shade of a teenager caught by his mother surfing porn.

My problem was that I hated confrontation, so I let her "help" me.

I shared that I was looking for someone who lived within forty minutes, enjoyed traveling, didn't smoke, had no small kids, was committed to a long-term relationship, sported no tattoos, had an average-slender build, and was 50 to 65.

The top five finalists for my bachelor's rose were all brunettes: two Asians, two Latinas, and one Black woman.

"Hmm," she said, peering over my shoulder.

I could tell she didn't approve.

Sure enough, she selected five others.

"What do you think?

What I thought is that she had a healthy opinion of herself. The women she picked out all looked like they could be her cousins.

"Look, if *you* want to meet one of them, fine," I joked, "But I'll pass."

Miffed by my wit, she backed up and huffed.

"I was being friendly. Forget about it. I have more boxes to pack."

She trudged back up the stairs.

I went back to my keyboard, sending out greetings and "hearting" women I found interesting on Zoosk, Plenty of Fish, and Match.

Smiling, I waited for my in-box to clog with messages from beauties flattered that a debonair man like me showed interest in them.

But as I sat there, the only note that came in was from a Ms. Onyeka, and I hadn't sent her a message or liked her profile.

She wrote to tell me her father died and left $3 million in her bank account. She couldn't withdraw it, but could with my help—and she'd give me $300k for my trouble!

Wow. Not this woman wanted to date me so badly that she was willing to *pay me.*

But then, *ah,* I told myself, remembering the tutorial with my online dating coach, Tom.

That's some tempting bait you're dangling, Ms. Catfisher—but no. And, besides, Nigeria is way outside the range of where I was willing to drive.

Delete.

I waited. If I could have played a soundtrack for the moment, it would have been Simon and Garfunkel's "The Sound of Silence."

That changed the following day, when my inbox *dinged* and *chirped* with hi's, hellos, and hearts from gorgeous females whom I never had contacted.

They were starting a conversation with *me.*

One looked like a blonde Victoria's Secret model, but with a better figure.

A second, a Latina in her upper twenties, sent a photo of herself in Santorini. It was mostly her, arched in a red bikini, with Greek scenery playing a minor backup role.

A third, a slender Asian woman, oozed sexuality, holding a glass of red wine, standing in pink golf shorts in front of a parked Porsche.

Hmm. I thought. *She can't make up her mind whether to drink, drive, or golf.*

Color me flattered, but confused. All three women were about thirty years younger than my profile said I was looking for.

"Single, lonely woman in a quest for a special man to travel with, dine, and love me 24/7. Age is not an issue," said one.

Contestant number two's message started with "Dear," then transitioned to typos and mangled sentences.

The third said she wanted to meet at a pricey restaurant in Los Angeles.

My thoughts drifted back to my Online Dating 101 class.

In my mind, I pictured the real face behind all three women: a three-hundred-pound guy in flip-flops chugging Cherry Coke from a liter bottle with gravy from his fries dripping on his keyboard. And all he/she wanted from me was a bank wire for a few hundred bucks to get out of an unexpected financial bind.

I passed.

Then, like finding a ruby in the rubble, I discovered one of the women I'd shot a note to had responded, May!

When I looked more closely at her profile, I noticed it was sparse, with a solitary picture and a few sentences that noted she was originally from Bangkok.

She said she was looking for a man my age or younger.

It excited me that she came from Thailand, the same land I journeyed to at the age of nineteen to begin my career as an Army broadcaster.

We exchanged texts and agreed to meet the coming weekend.

When Saturday rolled around, I opened the closet, grabbed a clean shirt, and paired it with wrinkle-free trousers.

Then, I slid into the final touch: the new shoes Shannon picked out for me.

The moment had arrived. I was about to go on my first online date. I felt like a pimply-faced kid venturing out to the senior prom—*tingly*.

Then I remembered why I felt that way. It was the Bengay I dabbed on my left knee.

Laughing at my forgetfulness, I tugged on my pants. A sharp jolt in my lower back further reminded me that I wasn't a teenager, just a sixty-two-year-old man trying to live like one.

Still, so what! A beautiful woman about twenty years younger than me wanted to meet.

Sure, all I had to go on was her picture, and the fact that she was Thai. But I'd get to know her in person.

What could possibly go wrong?

3. Love? Or Mango Sticky Rice?

One day back in May of 2016, I starred in "role reversal Saturday."

"I'll be back at ten, don't wait up for me," were words that should have been coming from my teenage daughter's lips, not mine.

But there I was, a vintage dad, calling out over my shoulder to Shannon as I went into the garage to squeeze into my Honda Fit.

The car sparkled. I maximized dazzle by waiting until date day to wash and vacuum it.

Thirty minutes before leaving, I showered. I splashed a few drops of Hai Karate aftershave behind my ear.

Clear for take off, I cruised down the highway going exactly sixty-five.

As I started my thirty-minute drive, my mind drifted to when I was a soldier.

Back then I was nineteen, about two years older than my daughter, and about to meet a Thai woman on a blind date in 1974—in Thailand.

My job was spinning vinyl as a DJ for the Army in U-Tapao.

Before joining, I hailed from a small Pennsylvania town where the biggest difference in people came from what shade of white the sun made you.

A few weeks into my tour, two of my work buddies brought me along to the beach resort of Pattaya to meet a gorgeous woman they knew.

"Trust me," said John, an Air Force Sergeant who fixed the broadcast equipment that journalists like me broke. "Once you meet Mallee, you'll never forget her."

When we piled out of the taxi after our ninety-minute drive, John handed the driver a carton of Marlboros. It was payment in full.

The sun had just gone down.

Beautiful women wearing very little lined both sides of the street, smiling from the front of scores of bars and restaurants.

John and my other buddies walked me into a bar called Phuket Let's Drink. As we walked toward an empty table, a woman called out to us. "Hey, GI!"

After we sat down and ordered a round of Singha beers, one of my coworkers, Phil, called a waitress.

"Would you call Mallee over?"

A few minutes later, a svelte, mocha, Asian *Sports Illustrated* swimsuit model look-alike swayed up to our table.

"Mallee!!" yelled my trio of friends. "Take a seat, and meet George—he's a newbie."

As we chatted, I couldn't believe it.

My first night in Pattaya, and I'd already hit it off with someone who seemed to be into me.

She was "I can't take my eyes off her" gorgeous.

Her only flaws—an odd voice and a big Adam's apple—were easy to overlook.

After about fifteen minutes of brushing up close to me, she whispered, "Want to come up to my room?"

Speechless, I turned to John.

"Man, we just met, but I can't believe how great we're getting along. She wants me to leave with her!"

"Did she say how much?"

"It's not like that," I said. "She likes me." Then I paused, letting his words percolate a bit in my beer-addled brain.

"What are you saying? She's a hooker?"

All three of my buddies and Mallee locked eyes on me.

"You know that song by Lou Reed, "Walk on the Wild Side?" asked Jan.

"Yeah, but . . . "

Then it hit me like a coconut falling on my skull. "You mean Mallee is . . . "

"A ladyboy," she said, finishing my sentence. "Come see what I have!"

Everyone except me erupted into laughter.

My jaw hung open like a PEZ candy dispenser. I passed on Mallee, the Thai with attractive packaging—but the wrong plumbing.

While there was no way I'd knowingly date a large Adam's apple variety of woman, I went on to meet some charming women in Southeast Asia. But it never clicked enough for me to propose to any of them.

Those romantic experiences were part of my immersion into Thai culture. I threw myself into the country's steamy hot weather, spicy cuisine, and the language.

Now, "2016 George" was minutes away from "going back in time" with May, a woman from a country I adored.

About ten minutes out from the Thai restaurant in Temecula, I replayed our online interactions.

When I first saw May's Zoosk profile, I saw a few photos of her posing in front of a temple I visited when I was a GI in 1974.

Sure, she could have been a tourist, but I didn't think so. My guess was that she used her real name on her profile.

She said she was forty-three.

Her profile listed no hobbies or interests, only her photo and the age range she'd accept: 18 to 99.

I'm well under her max age, I joked to myself. A "relatively" young fella. *I bet she found my handle funny—Can't Find My Keys.*

May responded to me right away, flattered that I spoke some of her language and had lived in her native country.

She declined a phone call, messaging me instead.

"My English isn't good. Let's text for now."

It was after a flurry of messages that we decided to meet at a restaurant.

In preparation for the date, I fished out my forty-year-old photo albums.

Leafing through the pages with crumpled corners, I examined yellowed images of me touring temples, riding in Baht buses, and posing with snakes. I looked younger and skinnier.

Despite the fact that the snapshots were more than four decades old, they were clear enough to tell my face from the python's.

Peeling off some Polaroids from the album, and fishing out some old Baht coins from a box, I placed my memories into a plastic bag and brought them with me to impress.

When I strolled into the Thai Me Up restaurant, I instantly recognized May sitting at a table.

Suddenly, there was a flash, like someone was jamming my brain with radio signals, and my thoughts wandered back to my introduction to the ladyboy in 1974 Pattaya.

Snapping out of it, and refocusing on the now, I felt guilty, but still glanced at her Adam's apple. *Whew.* It was feminine.

"Sawadee Cop, coon sabi dee mai?" (Hi, how are you?) I asked.

When May replied in Thai, I understood her first three words, but not the following fifty. She paused, smiled, and looked at me.

Her voice sounded all woman.

"Pom pood Thai dai nit noy May," (I can speak a little Thai)," I said.

She nodded, opened her purse, and fished out her phone. She typed fast, then angled her screen toward me so I could see.

May had written, "That's okay. Let's talk over food."

She was using a translation app! Now I realized why she didn't want to chat on the phone.

To "talk," I typed in a sentence, hit a button, and Thai words appeared.

Man, I told myself. *I expected awkwardness on a first date, but never imagined typing so much that my fingers cramped.*

"Why are you on Zoosk?" I asked. "What kind of guy are you looking for?"

When I posed the question, I'd already formulated a theory: her favorite color was green, as in the card.

Her fingers sprang into motion, producing an answer that did nothing to change my mind.

"I'm looking for a kind man to marry."

Part of me wanted to bail, but the other part wanted our meeting to continue. Our rendezvous beat watching TV alone at my apartment, crying into my leftovers, and muttering to the house plants.

Feeling like a TV reality show producer searching for content, I wanted to squeeze every quirky drop from the night.

Our date continued. She ordered a papaya salad. I chose chicken satay, Massaman curry, and a Singha draft.

We sat for about an hour typing and replying to each other on her phone. I showed her my photos from Thailand and a few old coins from 1974. She showed me some shots of her in Chiang Mai.

As we texted, May ordered and chugged beer like a dry well trying to refill itself.

She moved from sitting opposite me at the table to right beside me in the booth. It was then that she glanced down at my feet.

"New shoes?" she typed.

"Yes." I typed back.

"Nice!"

As I glanced at some snapshots of people spraying each other with Super Soakers and dumping pails of water on each other during the Thai water festival, she rested her hand on my knee.

Wow, I thought. *When I get home, I need to thank Shannon for the footwear tip.*

Then she messaged me a surprise request.

"Want to go dancing?"

When I nodded yes, she drained the last drops of her third brew, and she patted me gently on the arm.

Seconds after our in-person textathon began, I knew May would never be the new Mrs. Smith. But my libido had taken charge, determined to wear down my conscience to see things its way.

She wasn't "the one." May wasn't even a strong maybe. But what was wrong with mutually agreed on unbuttoning?

The waitress had long since cleared my plate. As we sat there, I opened my browser to search for a nearby drinking hole that might offer dancing.

A country place with a name that mixed attitude and fun popped up, The Sassy Saddle.

When we left the Thai restaurant, May reached for and held my hand. Opening the car door for her, I plugged the club into my navigation system.

Sassy's was only fifteen minutes from the restaurant.

While piloting my Honda, it struck me that the quantity of May's brewski intake had made me irresistible. Once again, her left hand wandered over to my right knee and lingered.

When I rolled up in the parking lot, my eyes widened. The place looked like someone had lined up three cargo containers, hung a neon sign out front, and called it a club.

Opening the door for May, I followed her in.

A whiff of wood polish and stale beer drifted our way. The lights were low. My eyes adjusted as I made out five guys sitting on stools in front of a large wooden bar. They all leaned forward, clutching bottles of beer.

The place featured five small tables crammed up against the opposite wall. I quickly figured out why they remained vacant.

Like honey bees drawn to a petunia, the men buzzed opposite Sassy's buxom blonde bartender.

The queen bee hypnotized the drones with long lashes and bright red lipstick. Topping off her look? A cowboy hat tipped upward just enough to accentuate her face.

"Welcome," she smiled, looking our way. Her admirers, following her head turn, did as well.

The room offered enough space for May and me to pull out chairs and sit at one of the tables. When I stretched out my arm, I could touch a wall with my extended fingertips.

Leaving May at the table, I walked over to order.

"What can I get you?" asked the bartender, without moving from behind her fortress of wood. It reminded me of a saloon from a Clint Eastwood western.

"A gin and tonic and a Diet Coke." I said, then asked, "Are you Sassy?"

"Yup. I *do* have attitude. My real name's Judy, but call me Sassy. I pour the drinks and own the place."

I smiled back as I waited.

"Your lady's not drinking?"

"Nope. The Coke's for me. I'm driving."

"Okay. No cost for that one."

She handed me the drinks. Picking them up, I walked over to May.

Throughout my conversation with Sassy, the guys at the bar occasionally turned my way, listening, but not saying anything to me.

A few minutes after sitting, May chugged her drink and texted, "Dance?"

While raising my finger to signal hold on, I turned, then walked over to the jukebox. Every selection was country.

The men sitting on stools had returned to flirting with Sassy.

Taking to the floor, I sent my limbs in random directions while moving my feet to the beat. My hips remained welded in place.

In the midst of my jerking like a chicken dodging a farmer's ax, May pulled me close and latched on like a barnacle. She pulled my shirt forward and looked down at my chest.

It embarrassed me more than it flattered. The only thing that popped into my head was I'd missed an opportunity for comedy gold. If only I'd remembered to glue on my fake chest hair toupee!

The banter at the bar softened to whispers. Sensing multiple eyes on us, I danced with my eyes riveted to my new fabric shoes.

My face felt hotter than the rest of my body. After a few more minutes of her public massage of me, I motioned toward our table.

After pulling out a chair for May, I walked over to Sassy to order another gin and tonic and Coke. Drink in hand, I pivoted to return to our table, only to get a jolt.

My date had snuck up behind me, purse in hand and was standing a foot away.

Without a word, she slid onto a barstool. I sat down next to her.

"Beautiful," cooed May to the bartender.

"Well, thank you, darling," replied Sassy, as my date drained half of her latest drink with a gulp.

"Very, very pretty," said May, standing up from her chair, leaning forward, and stroking the bartender's arm.

My dyed black eyebrows arched. My date—hitting on a woman?

It was bizarre. Did Sassy's hat conceal a hidden camera for some reality TV show like *Swipe Right, Cowgirl*?

My puckering peaked. The finger dance of May's frolicking fingers on a stranger snipped the last thread of my frayed patience.

Maneuvering my date back to her seat, I pointed to her phone.

"You've had too much to drink. We should go," I typed.

She looked at the translation, nodded, and drained her glass.

Motioning for Sassy, I settled our tab and left a big tip.

"Will she be all right?"

"She had a few before we came here, but she'll be fine," I said. "I'm taking her home."

As I opened my car door for her, May fished out her phone.

She took a long time to peck two words in Thai that translated to: "Your place?"

"I'm taking you home."

"No! No! No!"

We texted back and forth before I handed her phone back one last time, started up the car, and drove to where she lived—a small house she shared with two friends.

Neither of us said, or texted anything. The only sounds were the hum of the motor and the whoosh of cars passing us.

I glanced over at May. My pickled companion's arms were folded tight over her chest, accessorized by a scowl.

When we rolled up to the house, I walked over to her side of the car and helped her out. She slipped a bit, but I steadied her, walking her to her door.

"Okay?" I asked. No response.

When I rang the bell, an Asian woman about May's age answered. She spoke decent English.

"May had a bit too much to drink tonight," I said.

"Thank you," the roommate said, extending a steadying arm to May. My date still wouldn't look at me. She headed to the house like a canoe bobbing in the Pacific ocean. I turned, said good night, and left for my place.

When I pulled into the garage at eleven, I noticed Shannon had left a light on for me, but was asleep.

We chatted the next morning over breakfast on my first stateside date in decades.

"Sooooo, how was it?"

When I started to recount sitting next to May and communicating by translated texts, Shannon jumped in.

"Dad, you were out late. Why didn't the date end right there?"

As I told my daughter why the date lasted as long as it did, I couldn't believe the words tumbling off my lips.

Wanting to rekindle memorable times from Thailand? All right. But sticking around with a woman who spoke less English than a toddler? There was a simple explanation, but I didn't want to say it.

"Dad," Shannon said. "Come on. Why are you wasting your time on someone like that? She's not relationship material. Were you trying for something else?"

Pausing, and caught, I looked my daughter in the eyes.

"Sweetheart, all right. You're seventeen. Yes, I was. When I rolled up to her place, I was hoping she'd invite me inside and I'd score—some homemade mango sticky rice."

She laughed.

"Baby," I told my daughter. "I focused on her good looks and ignored a stadium of red flags. But look, what you're hinting at, nothing happened, honest. She got drunk, and I drove her home. On the positive side, she wasn't a Ladyboy!"

"A what?"

As I told my 1974 "war story" to my daughter, we laughed and, to my relief, moved on to tamer subjects, like how she was doing in lacrosse.

Later, as I replayed my first online date in my head, I focused on lessons learned:

1. Avoid women who only post a photo and no bio.
2. Call and talk with a woman before going out with her.
3. If someone gets handsy on the first date, chances are it's because I went up from a "seven" to a "ten" because of the drinks.

A week later, I deployed my index finger and commenced swiping.

Karen popped onto my screen. Unlike May, she described herself in complete sentences and listed hobbies, favorite movies, and dreams.

Little did I know, she craved something I wasn't willing to give.

4. Coffee and Chanel

The "textathon" disaster with May aggravated my arthritis, but I learned. Before meeting a date in person, start with texts, then call.

My prospects brightened when Karen, a night shift nurse working in the nearby city of Irvine, wowed me when we chatted one night right before her shift.

She had never married, put herself through nursing school, and saved enough for a down payment on a house. A bonus: she was an American citizen.

"She sounds great, Dad. Good luck," said Shannon, as I described Karen to her.

I squeezed in a few more minutes with my daughter while she waited for a friend to pick her up and drive her to the Temecula mall. Smiling, I said bye and boarded my fuel-efficient white chariot.

The bright June sun and blue skies radiated a positive omen as I drove from Murrieta to Irvine.

Fortunately, traffic moved. Some weekends, autos were backed up so much that walking backwards would have been faster, and way better for my creaky knees.

When I got out of the driver's seat of my leased Honda Fit, my joints sounded like someone munching on a bag of Ruffles.

Karen and I agreed to make our first face-to-face at Starbucks in the Spectrum Center: a safe public place.

I recognized her right away—a testament to her honesty. She hadn't posted old poses or photo-shopped manipulations. She was 5-foot-3 with long brunette hair, a slender figure, and a cute face.

"Karen?" I smiled.

"George? You look like your profile. A lot of men pull a bait-and-switch with an old pic, and show up fatter and balder."

Hmmm. I thought. *Her meeting "a lot" of guys threw up an amber flag. Was she picky, transparent, or addicted to putting another notch on her lipstick case?*

"I'm getting a Venti coffee latte," I said. "How about you?"

"The same," she smiled, placing a large, bulging Coach bag on an adjacent chair at our table.

While standing in line, a concentrated sound hit me like a thump on the chest. People's mouths opened and lips moved, but no matter how much I concentrated, I couldn't make out individual words.

The issue wasn't my hearing. It was a large number of humans squeezed into the place like coffee beans in a vacuum-packed bag.

A group of six kids who appeared to be students laughed, seated at two shoved-together tables near us. Each brought a laptop, but ignored it. Even *they* angled their ears close to each other to hear.

After grabbing our coffee, I squeezed between chairs, maneuvered to my table, and tried not to give strangers a baptism of java.

I think Karen thanked me for the drink, but amidst the din, I wasn't sure. Not wanting to yell, I scooted my chair close to her.

"Hold on," she said, showing me her palm and drawing back. "We just met."

"Okay," I said. "Didn't mean to send that kind of signal. I just want us to be able to talk without blowing out our vocal cords!"

We yelled some small talk for a few minutes when the table of six youngsters saved our voices by getting up and walking right toward the parking garage. Then some of the remaining crowd headed left.

I guessed they were headed toward the movie theaters. I noticed two of the teenage girls laughing, opening their bags, and comparing stashes of snacks.

"Phew," I sighed. "That's better."

It was then that Karen fished into her designer bag and pulled up three large albums—plopping them on the table.

It seemed to me she was angling her bag to make sure the Coach logo remained visible.

"Would you like to see some photos?" she asked.

"Sure," I said, wondering how the date morphed so quickly from "don't sit next to me," to "slide in close."

As I thumbed through the first album, I discovered every shot was of her. Karen with a Bentley or a Maserati. Karen in a bikini, or Karen lounging on a bed in a slip.

The toned and tanned woman looked forty, but was eleven years older than that.

"Lovely!" I said.

"Pick out your favorite ones," she said.

My mind shifted to panic. What kind of test was this?

If I only chose bikini and nightgown photos, would that make me look like a creep? If I picked the shot with the sports cars, did it mean I loved flashy wheels? If I passed on the maximum skin shots, did it mean I didn't find her attractive?

After careful thumbing, I announced two winners.

"No," she corrected. "Pick eight more."

Tearing off napkin parts, I marked my favorites and kept turning. After about fifteen minutes, I finished my homework assignment.

"Gorgeous," I said, "It's tough, but I selected two more shots from four categories: car, bikini, nightgown, and other."

"You're organized, George. Now, which ones do you think would work best on Zoosk?"

"Well," I said. "I was hoping we'd click, so you don't need to post any more photos. You could cancel your account."

"That's sweet," she cooed, "But pick the top five."

Karen acted like a saleswoman who wanted me to page through *Maxim* magazine, then go through it again before she asked me to sign up for a lifetime subscription.

Doubts crept in. What kind of person lugged snapshots weighing as much as a bag of flour with them on a first date? Why weren't they on her phone?

After what seemed like hours—though it was really only a few minutes—I paged to the five napkin pieces and pointed out the "winning" entries.

"Thanks," said Karen. "Are you up for a walk now?"

Her sudden pivot baffled me. Other than her initial greeting and compliment, she hadn't asked a single question about me. Thinking that might come later, I said "sure," thankful that show and tell was over.

We traded the coffee shop crowd sounds for the chirps of songbirds, the laughter of children, and the rustling sounds of people bustling past.

Relief coursed through my body. I guessed older people who glanced our way in the cafe imagined we were friends catching up, sharing memories.

The high school kids must have whispered under their breath, "Wow. That's what life before iCloud looked like. Rough!"

After a few minutes of strolling, Karen stopped and turned.

"Hey, let's go in here for a minute." She positioned herself outside Nordstrom's, waiting for me to open the door.

I did.

Little whiffs of rose, spice, and wood drifted to my nostrils as someone greeted us with "Welcome to Nordstroms."

I squinted and stumbled for a few seconds, blinded by a saleswoman readjusting a makeup mirror who unintentionally redirected sunlight at me.

Blinking, I followed my photo-album-loving acquaintance inside.

Why Nordstroms? And what was this? A sudden bathroom dash?

Karen, never breaking stride, zigged and zagged. I caught up to her in front of a display of Chanel No. 5. Snagging the 3.4 ounce size bottle, she pivoted to the cashier and handed it to her.

"That's $181 with tax," smiled the saleswoman. "Cash or card?"

Karen stepped back, positioning me closest to the cash register. She turned, smiled, and looked at me.

"Are you expecting me to buy this?"

"Why not?"

Hearing no response, she gazed at my face—blank and stunned, as if a vampire had drained every drop of blood.

"Too soon?" she asked.

Wow. I thought. *In a few hours, you've gone from "Don't sit so close" to "I want you to be my personal GoFundMe!*

The money miner passed on buying the fragrance for herself. Me? I was done.

Karen? She brushed it off.

As we walked, I glanced at my phone and came up with an excuse.

"Sorry, Karen, a text from a Mormon missionary friend of mine popped in. I forgot we have an appointment in ninety minutes. We're delving into the book of Jacob. I have to head back."

"But didn't you say you wanted some dinner first? They have great seafood near here."

"Not today. Let me walk you back to your car."

She glanced down at her shoes and agreed. As we strolled, she said her night shift nurse shift job made it hard to find the time to find the right guy.

Well, it's not just that, I thought.

After about five minutes, she stopped in the middle of a parking lot. I looked left and right for her Porsche, Lexus, or Tesla.

"Here we are," she said, gesturing to a used Honda Civic. The paint's clearcoat reminded me of my arms after sunburn—peeling.

The back seat was decorated with a mix of clothes and In-N-Out burger wrappers.

Karen got up on her toes and hugged me, as I managed an insincere smile and an awkward one-armed return embrace.

As I drove home, I pondered the experience. With my first acquaintance, May, our "comms" were knocked out, and I needed to retreat.

While language wasn't an issue with Karen, she made it clear she was searching for a two-legged ATM.

I didn't get it.

Nothing on Zoosk shouted, *"Welcome to George's profile, you've entered Venmo Valhalla!"*

She knew what I drove before we met. What about a dude driving a leased Honda Fit screams rich guy?

When I got home. I grabbed a drink and zipped over to check my computer for new dating prospects. I was certain Karen was doing the same. After all, I gave her coffee but no Chanel.

Time for more swiping.

Imagine my surprise when, the next night, my phone pinged with a greeting from Karen.

"Hey, George. What's up?"

Ignoring her message, I turned from my phone, back to my computer to continue looking for someone else.

"Why aren't you answering me?" she persisted.

Sighing, I took a sip of a delightful Italian cabernet I'd just opened, and thought about it. Ghosting her was cowardly.

I called her.

"Karen, we fit together like a peanut butter and liverwurst sandwich."

"That's a joke, right?"

Leveling, I said when she asked me to buy her an expensive perfume, I smelled trouble.

"I apologize," Karen said. "Please let me make it up to you. Let's start over. How about dinner? We can split the bill."

Pausing for a few moments, I mulled it over. It was a nice gesture. And, I was flattered that the pretty nurse wanted to see me again.

We agreed on a seafood restaurant in Huntington Beach and met in front of the place.

She dazzled in a mid-thigh white dress. Her long black hair flowed behind her as she smiled my way.

"Hi, I'm Karen. George?"

I laughed. The afternoon was off to a great start as we meandered behind our hostess toward our table overlooking the ocean. The day was a perfect 75° with a sweet, light breeze.

As we strolled, my eyes drifted over diners enjoying plates of crab, tuna, and salmon.

She chatted about the biorhythm challenges of working night shifts as a nurse, while struggling to remain coherent during the day.

"Well, I won't take it personally if your eyelids shut while I'm telling you about my week," I said, pivoting to me.

I told her about my job with the American Forces Network, answering complaints from troops overseas who wanted their team or political viewpoint on TV.

Karen interrupted me halfway through a story about a retired soldier poking fun at me because I went on TV with a Walmart red shirt and a matching red tie.

Raising an eyebrow, I stopped, curious what was worthy of her interrupting such a hilarious tale.

"George, I mentioned to my friends you didn't want to gift me the perfume. They couldn't understand why. One of them said she thought it's because you're cheap."

My mouth dropped open like a large mouth bass going for bait. As I stared, her pupils morphed into dollar signs.

She no longer struck me as beautiful. My appetite and patience were gone.

"Karen, I'm not the guy for you."

"Why, what kind of man do you think I want?"

"Someone who drives something classier than a Honda Fit."

Flagging down the waiter for the check, I paid for both of us.

Karen spoke up, "Don't you want me to pay for half?"

"No," I said. "I got it."

I wanted her to know I wasn't cheap, but I had a higher calling in life than becoming her personal GoFundMe.

My credit cards and bank account sighed in relief. The threat to drain them had passed.

As I drove home, I glanced in my mirror and laughed.

At least my early departure saved me from tacking on some extra pounds. Unwilling to choose between the baklava and tiramisu, I was ready to order both.

Replaying the date in my mind, I knew what Shannon would say if she were in the car.

"Dad, Karen's a genuine Karen. Why are you acting desperate? Why waste a second date with a woman like that?"

Yep, I didn't need to be with Shannon. My daughter was in my head.

Karen craved stacks of Benjamins, but all she would find in my pockets was a quarter I always carried for my Aldi supermarket cart.

I was disappointed. I'd hoped to find someone before I hit seventy. Reality had other plans. My quest hadn't hit a snag–it had just been rerouted. Somewhere out there, a new love was waiting–unaware of my timeline.

The first sign that a new date *could* be the one? She'd say "thanks" for the latte, without following up with a shopping list.

5. Is That Ectoplasm between Your Teeth?

The people who benefited the most from my dating worked at Starbucks or discount gas stations.

After my "dating for profit" lesson from "Karen Chanel," I turned hyper-picky, going out with a multitude of different women for five months.

I filled my four-wheeled white box with expensive fuel while buying a small pond of overpriced coffee.

When I met dates, it felt like we were interviewing each other for a job.

How long have you been dating?
How many are in your family?
What's your job like?

Once I tried mixing it up with humor:

Would you rather burp confetti or fart glitter?

She never finished her latte.

During my "speed dating" phase, if we didn't click right away, we'd say so over java then wish each other well.

Some relationships lasted a week or two before crashing in flames, often yielding "you won't believe what happened moments."

One time, a woman impressed me when I saw her gorgeous new two-floor home. It didn't phase me that her mom lived with her. What turned me off was how she managed life with her other "roommate," a black, miniature poodle.

When I walked into the wood floor living room, I saw her mom sitting on a fluffy chair with about seven sections of Bounty paper towels scattered around the room, wet.

"What's that?" I asked.

"Oh, Bosco (her dog) can't wait sometimes, so I just take care of it when it happens."

Take care of it, as in cover it and ignore it? Well, I thought, a bit relieved. *At least she's not cleaning up after her mom.*

Next!

Another date was charming. It didn't bother me that she was struggling with finances or that she lived with her adult daughter. It's just that the picture that formed in my mind when she told me this was nothing like reality.

When I visited her place, I found out she was renting one bedroom and a bath from someone who lived in the same house, and the room was so small that my date's bed and her daughter's were butted up against each other.

I'm a believer in staying close with my grown daughter too—but figuratively, not literally.

Resume swiping!

My next date, Mary, had an adult child who, fortunately, slept in a bed two hours away from her. He attended UCLA. Mary owned two homes, one forty minutes from me in Southern California, with the second a fix-me-up she'd purchased in Georgia.

Wanting to impress, I flew to the Peach State, booked a rental car, then drove to her place to help.

I was almost there when Mary called to say she'd be a bit delayed. She was off buying groceries.

When I pulled up in front of her place, I stared. The old red brick home sparkled. It looked like she'd power washed the exterior.

Comparing her place to the neighboring homes was like looking at an opal in a pile of coal.

Overgrown lawns were strewn with rusty auto parts, broken lawn chairs, and flattened toys. One home had boarded up windows, an open front door, and a couple sitting on chairs on the porch—seemingly unfazed by their surroundings.

As I looked around from inside my parked car, teenagers sitting on the opposite curb smoked and eyed the stranger in the unfamiliar car.

What made my wheels stand out was it had an intact windshield, no dents, and all four wheels.

It didn't take long for Mary to arrive. She drove up, saw me, waved, and opened the garage. She invited me to pull my Toyota in too.

When I got out of my car, a cloud of weed whacked my nostrils from the curb-sitting teenagers. They continued staring, only turning their heads when a mangy dog ran by chasing some kind of fast moving animal.

I hoped it was a squirrel.

Once inside Mary's place, my eyes widened. The home was immaculate. She had replaced the doors, kitchen, flooring, and cabinets.

"It looks great," I said. "But how are you going to sell it in such a run-down community?"

"I don't have to sell it for much to make a profit," she said. "It was a foreclosure. The bank was anxious to sell it."

Mary had little for me to do. All she asked was for me to haul some bags of renovation debris to the back of the house.

It was night when I started.

During the first load, I heard a rustling sound that I couldn't quite place. For a moment, I thought the yard was moving. It was a moonless night, and there was no back door light.

After taking out my last load, I fished my phone out of my pocket, turned on flashlight mode, and aimed it where I'd seen movement.

That's when my stomach contents started moving north. What I thought was grass was an undulating backyard of two-inch cockroaches locals called palmetto bugs.

I'm not sure how many were there, because I squealed like a startled piglet and bolted inside.

When I told Mary about the bug carpet, she shrugged it off.

"Oh. Yeah. You shut the door tight when you came in, right?"

It was clear it didn't bug her.

I pushed it out of my mind as well as we chatted that night over some salmon and a bottle of Chardonnay.

Then the wine and my naivety held hands, encouraging me to say words I later regretted.

"Mary, I believe in honesty in a relationship, and there's something I wanted to tell you."

"What's that, George?" she asked with understanding glistening in her eyes.

"I'm paying my ex-wife alimony. She'll continue to get it even if she remarries."

The glimmer in her eyes flickered–then went out, like a porch light nobody planned to fix.

"Thanks for the honesty, George. I don't know what to say about that. I need some time to think it over. I think it's best if you sleep in the guest bedroom tonight."

Man. I'd flown across the country only to get a time out.

In retrospect, it was way too early in our relationship for me to spring that burning cinder of information.

The next morning, Mary confirmed what I already knew.

"George, our relationship won't work out. No offense, but I feel you showed a lack of judgment. You should never have agreed to that alimony. It's putting you in a hole for the rest of your life."

Hmm. I thought. *I was getting this lecture from a woman who bought a house sight unseen—one with cockroaches that outnumbered the yard's blades of grass.*

As I flew home, I filed away my lesson learned and recalled a quote attributed to Mark Twain that fit me perfectly:

"It's better to keep one's mouth shut and be thought a fool, than to open it and remove all doubt."

As I resumed swiping, I suspected the reason I wasn't getting more nibbles: I was more of a Sequoia than a young sapling.

Still, living in a state of denial made me feel better.

I *imagined* some passed because they found my rugged good looks intimidating.

Perhaps others swiped left because I wasn't the "right cream for their coffee."

Or maybe people zoomed in on my profile picture and got turned off by the one eyelash that insists on growing three times as fast as the others.

Listening to my plight, a female friend offered advice on how I could instantly improve my appeal.

"George, there's nothing that turns a guy from a three into a ten faster than a big pile of money. Push that!"

It made sense, but I filled my bathtub with Mr. Bubble, not emerald dust.

Still, since I had a steady job, no debt, and money in the bank, I figured that bumped me from a five to a seven.

My challenge was creating a nuanced profile that communicated that I was financially stable and looking for a genuine partnership—not a member of Gold Diggers R Us.

One afternoon, scrolling through candidates on Match, I grinned. Someone sent a message to me before I sent one to her.

Jackie's large blue eyes reached out from the computer screen, fixing me in place. I rested my mouse.

She had short, brunette hair with just a hint of gray. Jackie described herself as Heinz

57, a mix of English, Italian, and Polish. She sported a medium build and was three years younger than me.

She posted a head-and-shoulders and a full body shot. Her hobbies included walking, reading, and traveling. She enjoyed some of the same music I did, including Selena Gomez, Taylor Swift, and hits from the '70s, '80s, and '90s.

Best of all, Jackie lived twenty minutes from me.

The only puzzler was when the app asked for a response to "religion," she typed a question mark.

Why not leave it blank, or not answer?

We decided to rendezvous at a Starbucks in the Southern California town of Temecula on a Saturday morning. The nearest school was a fifteen-minute drive away, so students didn't go there.

Learning from my cafe rendezvous mistake with Karen, I went to the place before the date. It was large, with many tables, and radiated a quiet, chill vibe. Most people grabbed their lattes and left.

It would do.

On the morning of our date, whiffs of warm cinnamon buns and coffee tickled my nostrils as I sauntered in. I glanced about. She sat at a table for two.

"Hi, Jackie! Up for a latte?"

After she nodded yes, I swiveled, went up to the cashier, and ordered two.

We sipped coffee and launched into small talk.

"So do you have any freaky dating app stories?" she asked, veering down an unexpected path.

I hesitated, said "well," then hesitated again.

She laughed.

"Let me explain why I asked and why I'm already happy to see you. On my last date, I was looking for a guy with brown hair, but couldn't find him. It was because in person he looked like Professor Xavier from the X-Men."

"Bald?" I asked.

"Yup. AND in a wheel-chair," she said, opening her eyes wide for dramatic impact, while shaking her head.

"I can't understand that," I said. "Why do people do that? It's obvious after you meet, AND it reveals a huge character flaw. They're lying."

Our exchange loosened the atmosphere.

She slid next to me, sipping on her java, and opened the dating app to show me a few of the men's profiles. One dude, Sexy69, posed in leopard skin spandex swim trunks, smiling in front of a small boat, with a glass of champagne.

Another fella, Man's Man, posed with a hunting rifle and a dead deer roped to his jeep with blood dripping from its mouth.

"They're peacocking," I said, showing off a word I'd only just recently learned from my friend Tom in Denny's.

"I'm guessing you're more of a coffee and pastry girl than a shoot, dress, and eat venison woman."

As we chatted, I opened my phone and a dating app to show some of my quirky interactions.

The first, a voluptuous early forties woman, posted a bio that led with, "Looking for a man who won't beat or cheat on me, with the financial strength to take care of me and my kids."

She wrote a four-paragraph blow-by-blow tale of enduring an abusive relationship with her boyfriend who fathered their three youngsters and still lived with her.

The woman's pictures on her bed and then lounging in front of a lit fireplace looked like a Victoria's Secret shoot, but sexier.

"What did her 'boyfriend' and 'her kids' do while the photographer snapped those shots with studio quality three-point lighting in their house?" Jackie laughed.

"Her story was so different from all the other online women that she made me look," I said.

"Classic clickbait," said Jackie. "Steamy pictures AND a story that makes you want to reach out and save her."

Jackie's eyebrows arched when I thumbed to the next two profiles on my app.

"Who are they, transgender?"

"Nope. They are 'dude dudes.' Someone hacked my account a few months ago. I got a message from Match that my new user name was Sue4Love. Imagine my surprise when I learned I now lived in Kentucky and was a fifty-four-year-old woman!"

"No way!" laughed Jackie.

"Yep, the scammer added two numbers to my email address and took over my account. For days guys from Kentucky messaged me telling me how hot they thought I was—but I'm *guessing* they were reacting to "Sue's" profile pictures, not mine."

Shaking my head, I explained that I still wasn't sure how exactly the scam was supposed to work. Match restored access to my account, but I still got occasional "likes" from guys—probably as a lingering result of the hack.

"Maybe your appeal is wider than you think," laughed Jackie.

Who was I to disagree?

Continuing on our shared theme of dating disasters, I shared my tale of Karen maneuvering me to buy her Chanel No. 5 on our first date.

That's when Jackie opened up even more.

"A guy, Sam, hit me up a few months ago. He listened and came across as patient and caring, but every time I suggested we meet, he had an excuse. He said he was a doctor who traveled a lot. One day, he texted me and said he was in Kenya with Doctors Without Borders. Bandits robbed him. He pleaded with me to wire him money for an airline ticket to come home."

"Typical scam," I said, sipping on my coffee.

"Yup, I said no. Messages stopped. Then weeks later, Sam, or whoever he is, sent me a new cry for help asking for cash."

We laughed, congratulating each other on our scammer radar. I went back to the counter and bought us each a muffin loaded with egg, cheese, and bacon.

When I sat down, I popped the question still burrowed in my brain.

"Why did you put a question mark after the religion block on your questionnaire?"

She paused, peeked down at her sandwich, and then leveled those magnificent blue eyes at me.

"You're Protestant, right?" she asked.

I nodded yes.

"I'm a spiritualist."

"What?"

"I believe everyone has a spirit. There's one inside you now. At any time, it could move to someone else."

"How do you know?" I asked, willing my eyebrows not to go into a full Mr. Spock.

"I'm a spiritual psychologist. I provide services to needy people around the world on Skype or Zoom."

I laughed. "If my inner being wanders from myself into someone else in between sessions, wouldn't you have to start over? Or bill me as two clients?"

"George, this is why I hesitated to bring it up. Most people don't understand and can't relate. We believe in integrating the mind, body, and spirit. Thoughts, emotions, and beliefs impact your health on a cellular level."

"Pardon me," I whispered. "Check your teeth. I think I'm seeing a bit of ectoplasm."

Jackie sighed, not amused. My sarcasm and one-liners strayed too far.

"It wasn't fair of me," I said. "I'm ignorant about that type of psychology. But I'm guessing you'll agree that with our differences, this won't work."

"You're right," Jackie said, glancing at a couple who'd entered the coffee shop holding hands. "Would you mind giving me a ride to a club down the street? My girlfriend is there."

"Sure!"

We left together. When I rolled up to the bar where her friend waited, I walked over to her door, and opened it. We smiled at each other, hugged, and parted. Little did I know, but there would be another psychologist in my future, and she'd be far more than a "meet, greet, and dash!'

My short time with Jackie was more directly honest than awkward. I revealed myself as a goofball, and she wasn't afraid to say who she was. Who knows, maybe she thought if she sat with me long enough, a spirit more empathetic to her would swap out with "cornball George."

During this, my speed date phase, I developed a simple nonverbal code with Shannon. After I got home, I flashed her a thumbs down. She turned back to her studies. No need for a long talk.

Man, I thought. Dating was a full-time job. It felt like déjá vu all over again. I woke up feeling like it was Groundhog Day. God hit rewind on my life. *Worst* of all, I was stringing together cliches with the same theme.

Disheartened but resolving to move forward, I pumped myself up. My "up to seven-year" odyssey hadn't yet yielded a new love, but it promised to be a hell of a lot more entertaining than hanging out with other gray hairs and yelling, "Bingo!"

Next up? A woman who offered a chance for me to take another dip into a culture I'd sampled and loved when I was a soldier in the 1970s!

6. Craving Kim(she)

One of the major *what-ifs* in my life was wondering what if I would have stayed in Korea longer to find love.

I re-enlisted twice to serve as an Army broadcaster in South Korea, 1975 to 1979, because the troops were appreciative, I enjoyed the gig, and the women were gorgeous.

Several times, I dated women who, given time, I may have married. The problem was my boss kept moving me from city to city to fill in for sergeants going back to the States on leave to see their wives for a few months.

Before leaving, they would kiss their Korean girlfriends goodbye and promise to be back soon.

A stewardess and I shared some passionate times together, but that ended when the Army sent me to Germany in December 1979, in the midst of a coup d'etat, which I didn't cause. Honest.

Fate granted me a second chance to see if my love of Korean food and culture would help fan the flames with a woman called Kim, who popped up on Match.

We differed in a way I was willing to overlook. I preferred classic rock, hip hop, EDM, and pop, while she enjoyed music by dead guys like Beethoven, Mozart, and Bach.

A professional cellist, she appeared as a solo artist in orchestras and taught private lessons. Kim was three years younger than me, held a four-year-degree, and had lived in the States for two decades.

We exchanged messages, and I told her I thought distance would be an issue. We lived about an hour and thirty minutes from each other.

"That's fine," Kim texted. "I drive past Murrieta on my way to give music lessons in Fallbrook. Let's meet on my way back."

"Let's do it," I messaged back on my app as I sat in Starbucks, chilling.

The latte joint was more than my top dating app meeting place. I'd show up solo to pitch myself to single women.

Full of confidence (or desperation), I dreamt that when an eligible woman heard one of my witty made-up names called out by the barista, she'd come over and ask me out.

Some of my favorites?

"Richen Single."
"Single N Lookin."
"Daddy."
and "Fire."

Even if my humor failed to land me a date, it made me smile to hear the high school-age baristas call them out.

My favorite reaction came when a young woman, caught up in the humdrum of her day, yelled out one of my coffee names without thinking.

"Fire," she said. Then, getting no response, yelled "FIRE," before the looks of startled customers shook her out of her daze before calling it out a third time.

When *I* was out of earshot, I'm guessing baristas exchanged nicknames for me, like Dad Joke, or Old N' Goofy.

Sipping my latte and once again amusing no one but myself, I sighed. Then inspiration struck with the eye-opening power of a triple espresso.

The coffee chain has long been a meeting spot for dating. What if Starbucks started selling personalized shout-out messages for people willing to pay a little extra?

Say you're a guy, Chris, who just met a woman, Sue, and you want to lighten the mood.

Slip the barista an extra five and have the coffee brewer call out, "A special order for Sue, from Chris. It's a cup of 'You're so beautiful you mocha me nervous.' "

Or, say you thought you were in an exclusive relationship with your steady, Cindy, only to find out she reactivated her dating profile.

Just slip the java jockey an extra Lincoln, and make up an excuse to go to the car.

That would be the cue for the barista to call out, "Cindy, he knows what you did, and he's not coming back. He ordered something that fits you— cold coffee."

Inspired, I searched the Starbucks website and submitted my glittery diamond of an idea. They never wrote back to thank me, or offer to pay for my innovative concept.

Despite getting crickets instead of cash from corporate, I remained a loyal client.

The following weekend, I met Kim at Starbucks.

"Hi," I said. "We meet at last!"

Kim smiled and asked me for a Venti Latte as I swiveled to place the order.

At ten a.m. on a Saturday, the place was about half full. Some guy who sounded like he was pitching life insurance was a few tables away, opposite an elderly couple.

Next to him was a woman with an open laptop, enjoying the free Wi-Fi.

Meanwhile, Kim was busy spicing up the small talk with me.

"When I was in my twenties in Los Angeles, I worked as a bunny for the Playboy Club!"

The old couple getting the insurance pitch turned our way.

The silver-haired woman choked on a sip of coffee. Her seventy-ish husband, who had already been sneaking glances at Kim, now locked on to her with wide eyes and a tractor-beam stare.

The woman with the laptop stopped in mid-type, with her fingers dangling over the keyboard, glancing our way.

"Wow, what was that like?" I asked, speaking for both myself and the nearby eavesdroppers, who had abandoned all pretense of not listening.

Kim shared stories of working in a tight dress with a cottontail. A big tip was often followed by, "What are you doing after work?"

She endured a torrent of rabbit and sex jokes. The top cliche—nice tail!

"Never went out with any of them," she said. "Dating a guy who hits on you in a bunny dress is no way to start a relationship."

"Well," I said, pivoting to my favorite subject (me). "When I was younger, I was objectified too. I was a hand model!"

"Really?"

"Yes. When women found out, they wanted to hold, caress, or help me moisturize."

Kim paused, then laughed. "You're joking!"

"Okay, fine—the true part is when I worked as an intern for Turner Broadcasting System's public affairs division in 2000, they used my hand—and a female co-worker's—for a handout brochure. But honestly? No one has ever used my 'modeling career' as an excuse to stroke my hand."

"Until now," said Kim, reaching over to hold my hand.

My brain chose that moment for a daydream.

I rewound to the late '70s and a date with my Korean Airlines stewardess girlfriend. Inexplicably, the date was on a flight bound for New York.

My seatbelt-enforcement officer (sweetheart) was telling me to let go of her hand; the man in seat 17A had turned on his call button.

But, no, it wasn't her. It was Kim in the present talking.

"You may let go now, George."

I started to respond with a quip, then thought better of it, granting my date complete freedom to do whatever she wanted—with her hand and mine.

"Kim, how about some lunch before you head home?"

"Sure!"

The two of us spent another hour together at a nearby Chinese restaurant.

Over the next few months, we went out once a week. Once, I went to one of her cello concerts. My friends Don and Sissy went too. We all enjoyed her company, dancing, and touring wineries in Temecula.

The couple were the parents of a close friend of my daughter, Shannon. Once again, I was struck by the irony of me dating at the same time as my daughter.

Shannon and I lived in a two-floor home in Murrieta, California. Four bedrooms and three baths made it way too big for two.

One night, trying to fill it up a bit more, I added one more person to the building's occupancy. I invited my new girlfriend to stay overnight.

Kim said she would leave the following day after breakfast for a private cello lesson about an hour down the highway from my place.

The morning after Kim's sleepover, all was going according to plan. I was making breakfast as she took out her cello and began playing in the living room at the base of the stairs.

Kim filled the house with deep bass and baritone notes as she pulled her bow over the strings.

As the scent of my sunny-side-up eggs and toasted English muffins joined notes of Beethoven in the air, the sounds of clinking coins grabbed my attention.

I heard Kim stop mid stroke and laugh.

It was Shannon. She'd come down the stairs and plunked a few nickels into Kim's open cello case.

My daughter and girlfriend both joined me in the kitchen for breakfast.

Shannon shared how she was adjusting as a junior in an American high school after living her entire life in Germany.

She talked about the friends she'd made, who all had international roots: a German-American, and exchange students from Spain, Norway, and Germany.

Kim talked about her son, one of the most accomplished cello players in California.

After breakfast, Shannon's friend Izzy swung by, and Kim left for her lesson.

That would turn out to be the high point in our relationship.

Soon, our rendezvouses started to feel less like fun and more like a full-time job. Kim's private lessons in Fallbrook ended, which meant I was no longer a convenient halfway stop.

I still made a few ninety-minute weekend drives to see her, but the long hauls were starting to wear on me—and that was the least of it.

Kim was about to tell me something that would completely harpoon our relationship.

The irony is that the fateful evening had actually started on a high note. I'd put on a suit and tie and driven to Lake Forest, California, to see her perform as a featured cello solo artist.

Kim was radiant in a glittery green sleeveless gown with a low back showcasing her slender physique.

I'd always wondered how a person who shunned the gym and avoided hikes managed to stay so toned.

The audience was about to witness far more than a solo performance—it was full on cello cardio.

As I sat in the audience entranced, her biceps bobbed and triceps thrust. When she leaned forward, shoulder muscles rippled.

Her face got into it as well, unleashing emotions that matched every note—eyebrows arched on the high ones, and her head dipped on the low ones.

She went into a blur of rapid bow movements that created a one-woman symphony of rich baritone, bass, and tenor notes,

The audience loved it as much as I did, giving Kim a well-deserved standing ovation.

I was impressed, and proud. She'd turned a pop music loving DJ like me into a classical music fan.

Afterward, we chatted over drinks and a steak dinner at an exclusive restaurant.

Just when I thought the night's performance was over, dinner turned into an unexpected second act.

After her third glass of cabernet, she looked at me with watery eyes.

"I was in love with the guy I was seeing before you."

Man, I thought. *Where's this going?*

Somehow, I succeeded in vocalizing a question.

"What happened with the two of you?"

"He gave me the key to his apartment," she continued, glancing down. "One night, I swung by to see him and caught him in bed with another woman."

Is this when she tells me she thought it over and she's going to start driving to my house again?

I decided a little levity might ease the awkward situation.

"Maybe she was a door-to-door sheet sales rep who wanted to demonstrate the quality of her merchandise."

"That's not funny."

She was wrong. It was hilarious, but I kept that to myself and asked, "What happened?"

"He told *me* to leave and put my key on the kitchen table on the way out—but I left and kept it."

Ah, so this is the part where she transitions to how grateful she is to have an upgrade of a boyfriend like me, instead of a cheater? Nope.

"I came back the next night, opened the door, and found him in bed with her again!"

"Are you sure she ever left the bed?" I laughed. "Sounds like a love marathon."

Kim didn't smile. She was in a kind of trance. It was like she was talking to herself and I wasn't there.

Finally her eyes lost their glaze and she focused. I guessed she wanted me to say something.

"Uh, Kim, why are you telling me this?"

"Because I still love him!"

That was it. She said she was in love with a guy who cheated on her twice in two days and told her to leave. Despite that, she didn't get the hint that it was over between them.

I did. We broke up.

Shannon took the breakup harder than me, but not because she missed Kim. It was because of a pattern I'd settled into that impacted her.

That came out one weekend when I brought a different date by the house. My daughter was polite, but distant.

Afterward, I asked her why.

"Dad," she said. "Please only bring someone to our house if you're serious about her, *then* introduce me. Are you good with that?"

A mixture of surprise and embarrassment bubbled up inside me.

"Sweetheart," I replied. "I understand. It's not fair to you. It won't happen again. This is your house too."

"Instead of dating apps, have you tried meeting someone another way?"

"Well," I told my teenager, "The church holds a seniors' singles group get together. Maybe I'll give it a try."

The following weekend, I showed up at an outdoor barbecue hosted by the church, a five-minute drive from my house.

As I strolled toward an open fire pit, a large BBQ grill grabbed my attention. A cloud of grilling hot-dog and hamburger smoke drifted my way.

About thirty people chatted around an open-pit fire or by picnic tables. The ratio of three women to each man looked promising.

My guess was that most of the people were in their forties or fifties.

While Southern California has lots of flavors, a quick scan of the group revealed lots of vanilla, no chocolate, and three mochas.

I was a plain vanilla, wearing a pair of neat jeans with a light blue polo. The others were *French* vanilla. They were slim and bronzed, with tasteful gold chains, and expensive-looking shoes.

I hoped none of them focused on my Honda Fit.

Shuffling up to the grill, I ordered a hamburger.

"It's good you're ordering one of those," smiled Senior Ken, who talked with me but kept one eye on a nearby Senior Barbie. "The veggie burgers are all gone."

Observing, but not speaking, I slid onto a vacant spot at a table. Three women sat at the opposite end chatting.

They were *managed*. I'd call them Venice Beach French vanillas. They had a light dusting of cosmetic surgery without making it seem like they'd rolled straight off the same assembly line.

Glancing their way, I munched my burger. A bit of mustard dribbled onto my chin.

"Hi, new guy," said one woman. "Want to join us?'

Nodding yes, I moved over, dabbing my chin with a Kirkland paper napkin. We chatted a bit about the church, and our mutual respect for head pastor John and his wife Anne.

"Do you like to travel?" I asked.

One of the women, Jill, spoke up.

"Sure. I've been all over California."

"Anywhere else?"

"Naw. California has it all—swimming at Huntington Beach, skiing at Big Bear and spas in the desert at Palm Springs. Why leave?"

Jill's companion, Arlene, disagreed a bit.

"California's great, but Nevada's nice too. I visit my son in Vegas all the time. The drive's beautiful."

"Have any of you ever been out of the country?" I asked.

The third woman, Sally, said she had been to Haiti.

"Why Haiti?" I asked.

"I flew there for two weeks on a mission with the church. It's a depressing place."

Since no one asked where I'd been, I volunteered.

"Utah's gorgeous. I hiked the slot canyons and the Zion National Park area."

Glancing over at Jill, I observed the impact of my words: her eyes looked like an early frost was settling in.

She started glancing away from me and at the burger-flipping man.

"You'd enjoy Europe," I said to the trio. "When you walk through the Swiss Alps, breathe in the mountain flowers, and gaze at those carpets of green grass, you'll think you're in a Heidi movie."

Now I'd lost Arlene. She was looking my way, but over my shoulder. I half turned.

Behind me stood a guy who looked like a Greek statue wearing khaki shorts.

"It sounds like none of you are interested in international travel," I said. "Why not?"

My direct question pulled their wandering eyes and minds back into the conversation.

"My kids both live in California. I'd rather visit them and my grandbabies," said Sally as the others nodded in understanding.

Wow. I thought. *Grandchildren? I can't relate to them there. I don't have any. And, to them, I'm like a three-legged male from Alpha Centauri.*

No one related to or showed interest in any of my life experiences.

My forty years of living overseas in Korea, Thailand, and Germany were as riveting to them as standing in line at Costco for rotisserie chicken.

The only place I experienced more red flags was Tiananmen Square on May Day.

The church ladies and I made weak excuses to each other as we peeled off in different directions.

Driving home, I reflected.

I enjoyed growing up in an almost all white small community in Pennsylvania in the '60s and '70s.

While I cherished my time there, and enjoyed going back to visit, my decades of living and working overseas made me thirsty for people who shared my love of travel

I wanted a wife who, like me, found differences in culture fascinating, instead of a turn-off.

While some of my friends were happy living in the town they grew up in, I wanted something different like snorkeling in the

Polynesian Islands, driving across the Outback in Australia, or chowing down on paella in Spain—all with someone special.

After a year of dating, the only thing I had to show for it was caffeine addiction and balding tires.

But it wouldn't be right to stop now! I told myself. *Keep trying until you hit seventy!*

For the moment, I chose to model myself after Johnny Appleseed, but with coffee beans. I'd travel throughout Southern California dispensing free joe to single women.

My new nickname? *Georgie Coffee Cup.*

7. Gray Wolf Seeks Mate, Pup in the Den

At times, I felt like a gray wolf who lost his mate to a poacher, padding about Southern California on dates, with a cub still in the den.

Battling guilt, I sipped coffee with strangers while Shannon spent time with friends.

As an older, and presumably wiser person, I wanted to have a dad-to-daughter talk about dating.

The problem? My lasting relationship credentials were as impressive as Elon Musk's.

Who was I to dispense advice on dating when I needed a co-worker to give me a crash course on apps?

And my track record? The women I'd met? Not only had I failed to find a good match, but it seemed that the very molecules in their bodies and mine required social distancing.

And, while my lifetime as a man gave me a wealth of male insights, there's only so much a single dad can offer.

Shannon recognized I was trying. One Mother's Day, she handed me a frilly pink greeting from Hallmark with a Sharpie that added the letters "d-a" to Mom.

"I love you, Momda!"

Battling my insecurities, one night I decided to father up and discuss her dating life. She had been seeing a guy named Brad, her first boyfriend, for months.

He hadn't been coming by the house as much, and I was curious how they were doing. I also wanted to chat about the following week's visit of three of her girlfriends from Germany. They were staying at our house for a month.

Hints of cumin and turmeric lingered in the dining room from my home-made chicken curry. As I passed the chutney, I glanced at my daughter.

"Do you like it, Shannon? I got the recipe from someone I'm dating, Phatsara. She's Thai."

"Dad, I'm glad you're seeing someone, but will you make some time to take us around when my friends visit?"

I knew where she was going with this. My daughter hadn't passed her driver's license test yet.

Smiling, I told Shannon I'd taken off two weeks from work and I would drive her and her buddies to all the beaches, malls, and amusement parks we could cram into the time they were with us. Phatsara wouldn't be my priority.

"By the way," I asked, "How's it going with Brad?"

"Dad, I really don't want to talk about it."

It took my daughter less than five seconds to shoot down my "let's talk dating" trial balloon. In my mind, I saw it crash with a plop into the chutney, making a yellow ripple.

A few days later, Shannon and I took off in my trusty Honda Fit to meet her friends Meli and Denise at Los Angeles Airport (LAX). Her other friend, Franzi, had already arrived.

"Guten Abend (good evening)," I said as I greeted the seventeen-year-olds, who were dressed like they were expecting to leave the terminal and step right onto the beach.

They sported shorty shorts, designer sunglasses, and belly-button-revealing "I 🖤 LA" T-shirts.

As we drove, I glanced back in the back seat. It looked like they collectively formed a Luggage Transformer robot creature. I couldn't tell where they ended and their bags began.

Once we rolled up to my two-story house, space wasn't an issue. While I had two spare bedrooms, they all wanted to stay with Shannon in her room.

The Germans had only been with us for a few days when Shannon suffered heartbreak. She and Brad broke up.

Having her childhood friends with her when it happened couldn't have worked out better. It was like crying through a sad movie with friends who came and shared tissues and Lowenbrau.

The most important thing was that when Shannon needed *me*, I was in the house with her, not out on a date.

Thinking fast, I asked my daughter to bring a few of her ex's photos outside to the edge of our pool.

That night, each of the girls and I said what we admired most about Shannon. Then we each sounded off about Brad. Since he loved golf, my story was:

"Brad is such a loser, he was on the third hole when Shannon showed up in a bikini—and he kept playing golf."

We soaked her canceled boyfriend's picture with butane and torched it. Fiery flecks of his face flew into the night.

The next day, California sunshine and the pool and jacuzzi helped soften the heartbreak.

The girls and I crammed into my stubby white car. A glance into my rear-view mirror revealed a new look for the girls.

They were part German, part towel, and part inner tube.

As we drove the hour and twenty minutes to La Jolla, the conversation turned to my quest to find new love.

"Found anyone yet?" asked Meli.

"Well," I replied. "I just started seeing a woman named Phatsara, but it's too early to say where it's going."

"That's an unusual name," said Meli. "Where is she from?"

"Munich. She's a nice German girl. You should see her in a dirndl (old-fashioned German dress)!"

The girls laughed. From the name, they'd already figured she was probably from an Asian country. They just weren't sure which one.

The image of Phatsara wearing a "milk the cows" Alps outfit wasn't something they expected.

"I'm always looking for a new and improved George 2.0," I said to the girls. "What tips do you have?"

It was a sign of how desperate I was for advice. There I sat, asking for dating advice from a car full of seventeen-year-olds.

"Be yourself," said Meli, adding, "Joke around. And be straight with them."

"You should shop with me," Franzi chimed in. "Buy some new clothes!"

"What's wrong with what I'm wearing? People will think I'm a designer, George, from Walmart."

No one laughed. In retrospect, they probably never heard of Walmart. Even if all their luggage was lost from Germany, there was no way they'd walk into the store. Instead, they'd rather squeeze into some of Shannon's old clothes I'd boxed up for Goodwill.

The next day, I drove Shannon, Meli, and Denise to Six Flags. Since Franzi didn't enjoy roller coasters, the two of us went to the Valencia Town Center mall for a few hours.

At her suggestion, I snagged a pair of Air Jordans, then Hollister shirts and jeans.

As I tucked my T-shirt into my jeans, Franzi spoke up.

"No. Don't do that. That makes you look like a grandpa."

I harbored doubts about accepting fashion tips from a teenager, but did it.

Hours later when we got home, in the midst of my bonding with the teenagers, Phatsara called and asked to stop by the house.

"Let me help you with the kids!"

I agreed and slipped on my new Hollister jeans and shirt, and Air Jordans before she showed up.

"Nice shirt," said Phatsara, carrying a huge bag of cartons of Pad Thai, spring rolls, Panang curry, and rice.

I sliced up a huge watermelon, a treat Meli loved so much we called her "Water Meli."

Once the kids heard Thai food was on the table, they jumped out of the pool, toweled off, and hurried in.

"Mffbbww," said the hungry teens, shoveling in food, forming a series of sounds that might have been "thanks," "delicious," or "hey, that's mine!"

After a few minutes, I thanked Phatsara for stopping by with food and promised I'd spend more time with her once I returned the kids to LAX for their flight to Frankfurt.

She smiled, said she understood, and would hold me to it.

That night, as I lay in bed alone, spotlights lined my path. For the last few months, I'd been "all in" on dating and hadn't spent enough time with my daughter.

I lacked balance. Before wandering from my den, I needed to check in with my "cub," and most importantly, be there for her when it mattered.

To this day, I still fondly remember being one of the shoulders for her to cry on when she and her first boyfriend split.

Lying there in my Chewbacca onesie, I smiled, knowing my decision to take a momentary break from dating was the right one.

In the future, the gray wolf resolved to fence off more quality time with his cub, and respect that the den was ours, not just mine.

Unbeknownst to me, though, Father Time planned to ambush me on my future path, threatening my life and my quest.

8. Thai Me Up

The German girls' one-month visit filled our house with joy and watermelon. That's what I told them as I piloted my Honda Fit toward LAX.

About thirty minutes from the terminal, traffic slowed.

"Dad, forget Waze," Shannon said, pointing up to what I perceived as a fuzzy shape. "The ramp is closed for construction. We need to follow the detour signs."

"I'm looking at a diamond-shaped sign," I said, squinting, "but it's too dark. Where are the street lights?"

"Dad, are your eyes playing hide and seek?"

"It's up ahead," joined Meli. "Turn left."

Fortunately, I always add some extra time to a trip to the airport. We arrived at the departure terminal with time to spare.

I hugged each of the girls and invited them to come back anytime. Each arrived in the States with one empty suitcase, and left with it brimming with outlet store clothes and shoes.

As Shannon and I drove back home, we chatted about what a special visit it was. The timing for their visit couldn't have been better. When my daughter and her boyfriend broke up, her girlfriends loved, cared, and related to her as only fellow teenagers could.

In the days to follow, our food lasted longer, and the house turned quieter. Shannon went back to school.

I trudged back to work and flipped my thoughts back to dating.

It was time for me to transition back to a single-and-ready-to-mingle mindset with the woman I met right before Shannon's friends came to visit—Phatsara.

"Did you say Fat Sara?" laughed my son, Brandon, home from college. "Why don't you just call her Sara? You're no Slim Jim yourself, Dad!"

He was joking. But the line burrowed into my brain. I prayed the nickname would never sneak out in the midst of a conversation with her.

Days later, I phoned Phatsara, and, thankfully, the pun stayed buried as I asked her to pick a place to go the following weekend.

"Want to check out a Thai temple?" she asked.

"Sure, but I can't take the vacation time right now for a trip to Bangkok."

"No, " she laughed. "Let's drive to one about thirty minutes from here."

It shocked me. A Thai temple in California? As it turned out, several dotted the suburbs around us.

After about twenty-five minutes on the

highway, we exited and started taking a series of turns in a rural area.

After driving for ten more minutes, the image of the blue road line turned white—Waze talk for "I'm lost."

Phatsara took over and verbally navigated me onto a dirt road lined with shrubs and tall grass.

As we completed a hard right past a half-dead pine tree, a sign in Thai popped into view.

I glimpsed bright flashes of gold, red, white, and yellow through the brush.

Our bumpy ride ended in an area with compacted sandy California dirt. I pulled in between two parked cars, both coated with brown dust.

When I opened my door and examined my roof, it sported the same grime.

As we walked by hedges, scratching and clucking sounds reached my ears. Rounding the corner, I saw a yard full of chickens. They patrolled rows of herbs and vegetables, pecking and clucking in a search for food.

The area was lined with some kind of tree I didn't recognize, bursting with small orange fruit the size of olives.

Phatsara picked off a colorful one and popped it in my mouth.

"Try it!"

"I eat the peel?"

"Yes. And seeds too."

It puckered like a lemon with the aftertaste of an orange—tart and juicy, a kumquat.

We ended up in front of the temple.

I'd seen scores of Buddhist worship places when I was a soldier in Thailand from in the mid '70s. I gazed in wonder at the reclining Buddha, Jade Buddha, and Emerald Buddha, and a smaller temple. But I'd never seen one in the United States.

The musky scent of incense drifted our way.

Phatsara asked me to wait a moment. She came back with an orange-robed bald guy who seemed like he just stepped off the set of *Avatar: The Last Airbender*.

I greeted him and introduced myself in Thai, resisting the urge to ask if he had the firebender ability, and if so, if he'd mind heating up some tea.

The monk gave me a gapped smile, complimented me on remembering some Thai, and invited us in. We pulled off our shoes.

Phatsara clasped her palms together in front of her chest and bowed her head. I did too.

After about five minutes, we got up, left, and sat at a small wooden table some thirty feet from the temple. Phatsara asked if I minded donating some cash to the monks.

"No problem. I'm a veteran at this kind of thing. When I was a kid I put an envelope on the offering   plate at Centenary Methodist Church every Sunday. It wasn't until later that I found out the lay leaders didn't appreciate it."

"Why are you bringing that up now?"

Well, the reason was it reminded me of a funny story from my past that I was *certain* would charm her. I continued.

"I'd cut out paper circles, print 'one Polish nickel' on it—or 'IOU a dollar'—stick it inside, and seal it. When I left the church for the Army, the lay leader got in front of the congregation and said he was glad no one was doing that anymore."

With the story complete, I paused, waiting for my reward—a laugh. It never came.

"Well, I hope you didn't do that with the monk," Phatsara said, half seriously, but with a tone in her voice revealing her suspicions that I might have.

I assured her that the childish part of my past was *mostly* over, and I hadn't slipped the orange-robed baldie an IOU.

Visiting the temple stirred up happy memories from forty years prior, when I was a wide-eyed teenager in Thailand.

After we left the temple, Phatsara and I went on to spend more time together.

Eventually, I invited her over to my house. While Shannon accepted her, they never formed a connection.

Whenever Phatsara visited, I cleaned the house while she played Thai music and TV shows from her iPad.

Listening to the songs as I worked reminded me of my youth, strolling through an outdoor market in Bangkok, with merchants selling coconuts, incense, paperbacks, and spices. The vendors played music like hers while they waited for a paying customer.

My current day girlfriend believed in odd superstitions.

When I showed her my collection of paintings from Thailand, Korea, Japan, and the Philippines, I thought she would compliment me on my style and appreciation of Asia. Nope.

"They spook me," she said, eyeing an oil from Filipino Artist Roger San Miquel.

The oil featured two young women in traditional straw hats cradling arms full of rice stalks. The canvas glowed, rich with hues of orange, yellow, and brown.

"What bothers you?" I asked as she continued to motion to other art.

Phatsara pointed to my three-foot-tall Japanese watercolor painting of six women in kimonos sketching inside a two-floor ancient home, and a realistic oil of a Korean woman holding a traditional instrument while wearing a long formal pink dress decorated with cranes.

"I believe when you have paintings with people on them, spirits may use them as a resting place."

"So, you think my art comes to life like in the movie *Night at the Museum*?" I asked.

"Are you making fun of me?

"Well, just a little."

What I didn't realize was that Shannon was in the next room reading. She overheard our conversation.

After Phatsara left, we sat down for some pizza and a chat.

"Dad," Shannon asked. "Other than she's pretty, what do you see in her? You like classic rock, pop, EDM, and cello solos. She likes music with drums, flutes, and cymbals. You're Christian. She's Buddhist!"

"Well," I replied, "She cooks great food and she walks on my back during massages!"

"Too much information."

"Shannon, I'm sixty-three. It's hard to find someone who has everything I want."

"Dad, don't settle for anyone. You're funny, smart, and handsome."

She's your daughter and she's biased, said my inner voice.

While I agreed with "inner me," eventually Shannon's words of warning rooted and grew.

The next week, I visited Phatsara at her place on a Saturday afternoon. She told me the home was her ex-husband's, but he let her use it.

"Do you mean you got the house after the divorce?" I asked.

"No," she replied. "He said I could stay here, not have it. I don't want anything from him."

It struck me as odd. Which was it, hers or her ex-husband's?

The question evaporated from my mind once I sat down for supper. Phatsara made a delicious lunch of papaya salad, rice, and spring rolls.

"All the time I was in Thailand, I never tried papaya salad. What's in it?"

"Shredded green papayas, peanuts, scallions, and other goodies!"

We were chilling after lunch when Phatsara hit me with some words that brought the Singha beer in my hand to a slow boil.

"George, we've been seeing each other for about three months now. I have a question for you. It's important for me to understand if you're financially stable."

"Don't worry," I replied. "The only debt I have is the mortgage on my house. I have a steady job with the federal government, cash in the bank, and stocks."

"Would you show me?"

"Come again?"

"I believe you, but I've dated guys before who say they're doing well, but they're not. May I see your bank statements?"

I inhaled, paused, thought about it, then, channeling Ronald Reagan, said, "Sure—trust but verify. How about we show each other our bank statements?"

She responded without a pause, almost

as if she had previously held a similar conversation with someone else and was prepared with what to say next.

"I'm doing fine," Phatsara said. "You don't need to worry about me."

I was flabbergasted. In one conversation, Phatsara morphed from girlfriend into IRS auditor.

Deflecting, I made small talk for another thirty minutes to avoid more discussion on money. Then I kissed her goodbye and headed home.

Over the week, I dissected her request, trying to examine it through her eyes. I suspected she met plenty of liars who would overpromise and underdeliver.

From my side, her request insulted me.

What's next? I thought—*her asking a certified public accountant to review my accounts?*

Chanting "om" three times, I chilled with a few minutes of breathing exercises. I decided to swing by her home, say "no" to providing the financial records, and try to rekindle my romantic feelings for her.

We started with a light lunch of Panang vegetable curry and rice.

I brought along some snapshots of my time in Thailand. She fished out one of her photo albums.

We were laughing and comparing photos when I spied a familiar face in one of her snapshots: Phatsara laughing with May, the Thai woman I dated for one eventful night who knew less English than a smart one-year-old, preferring to communicate via a translation app.

"We went on a date," I said, grabbing the photo and pointing at the woman whose "communication" made my fingers cramp.

Phatsara's eyebrows moved skyward. She reclaimed the photograph, buried it in her stack of already viewed prints, and tried to change the subject.

"Have you ever been to Chiang-Mai? I used to live there."

"Hey, it's no biggie," I said. "I went out once with May. It didn't work out. She spoke no English. Are you friends?"

"She was looking for a place to stay when she came here from Thailand," Phatsara said. "She stayed a month, left, and moved into a house with some other Thai women. But her real name is Sudarat. She's searching for a husband, but she's not a good woman."

"Why?"

"Because she's married, with a husband in Thailand."

Man, the one-date texter's profile name should have been Two Husbands R Better Than One. My lips started to form more questions when the downstairs door opened.

Phatsara called out in Thai as a tall young man strolled into the living room.

"Somchai, this is George," she said.

"Hi," I replied.

"Somchai works at a Thai restaurant as a cook. His two brothers do too," she said.

"Oh," I said. "Where are they?"

"They work later, they'll be home in a few hours."

"You all stay here together?" I asked.

"Yes, they each have a room."

Hmm. I thought. *The tale gets even more peculiar. Not only did she live in a house that wasn't hers, her three twenty-something adult sons did as well!*

She had previously shared that she had three adult boys, but I assumed they each had a place of their own.

We went through a few more photos when my girlfriend again brought up my financial records.

"Phatsara, I hoped you'd drop that. I didn't want to talk about it last time. And now, you're asking a second time. We're not a good match."

She spent another five minutes trying to convince me that proving my net worth was normal. Women had to be careful they weren't being lied to or scammed by men who weren't who they said they were.

"I understand, Phatsara," I said, even though I didn't. "'I'm sure you'll find the right guy, but it's not me."

I hugged her good night and went home.

Soured by the experience, I rested my online dating for a few weeks. I focused on my job.

I still exchanged phone calls with Phatsara as a friend. She shared that she changed her name to Noi.

"How can you do that?" I asked, "Do you have to sign some legal documents?"

She laughed, "I didn't ask permission, I just did it."

Noi, a.k.a. Phatsara, confided that she was dating someone new. The calls dribbled to a stop.

A few months later, Noi's face popped up on Facebook. She'd posted wedding pictures with a dude wearing a huge cowboy hat and boots at his ranch. She wore a matching set.

I wondered if "Tex" moved into the "house that wasn't hers" along with her lads, or moved everyone to his place. Moving them to his ranch would've been the smart call. He'd score a four-for-one special: a wife and three farm hands who could cook.

For me—bullet dodged.

Meanwhile, my dating life had slowed. I felt like a thirsty man crawling in the desert, searching for water, only to find nothing but cacti.

Months later, I was driving my Honda Fit toward my work vanpool pick-up point on a Monday morning at 4:45. Light fog was lifting from the road.

Going about 45 mph, I peered ahead, squinting at an odd sight: a faint line of orangish lights.

Cool! A UFO landed on the highway. Perhaps a voluptuous seven-foot blue alien woman saw my profile, and had a thing for pale "short" 5-foot-10 guys, and wanted to meet!

Nope. I was viewing the trailer of an eighteen-wheeler from the side. The driver had turned the cab down the road.

There were no headlights or brake lights to warn me of the danger ahead, only the dim lights of the trailer covering both lanes of the two-lane highway,

By the time my brain registered what was happening, I had no time to brake. Swerving my subcompact into the opposite two lanes of oncoming traffic, I panicked.

My little wheeled box was the wrong vehicle for bumper cars.

My eyes opened to saucer size. I clutched the wheel, trying to avoid oncoming traffic and steer to the side of the road. I failed.

Thump, whump.

A truck hit me head-on, pushing me out of moving traffic to the side.

My front and side airbags deployed. The impact tossed me like a salad into the driver's side airbag as my shoulder bore the brunt of the crash.

When the police came, I groggily focused on the pancake that used to be my car.

Thank God the crash hadn't transformed me into syrup.

The truck turned the driver's side of my car into a metal Twizzler. Luckily, the passenger's side was intact enough for me to crawl out.

The truck that hit me? For him, it was like a ladybug had hit the bumper and left a smudge. The driver was fine.

Later, I discovered I had avoided a double threat to my life.

The airbag was a Takata, which was responsible for at least twenty-eight deaths in the United States and more than four hundred injuries.

Shortly after my accident, the airbag was recalled for deploying and spraying metal shards. Mine didn't. It puffed up like a giant marshmallow and saved me.

A week later, while undergoing a physical, I found one reason I didn't see the tractor-trailer making a slow turn onto the highway—I had cataracts.

When Shannon and her friends laughed at my inability to see signs when I drove them to the airport, it was an early indicator I missed.

God was telling me to get my half-blind ass off the highway and go in to visit a doctor.

Shannon was also right when she told me Phatsara and I had as much in common as toothpaste and Tylenol.

The scoreboard lit up: Daughter two, Dad zero.

The car accident Father Time threw at me was a major setback. Had I updated my profile right then it would have read:

Seeking a woman to nurse me back to health. Since I can't see well, looks are unimportant. And oh, my car's wrecked and so am I. Can you pick me up?

While I tried to gaze into the future with an optimistic eye, it was tough with cataracts—everything was blurry.

Still, I was no quitter. I resolved to continue my quest to find new love before seventy—right after a short intermission.

The Great Clockmaster ambushed me, and I survived. But I needed a body shop, and one for my car too.

9. Chassis Realignment

After taking a U-turn on the highway to heaven in 2017, I felt as physically and mentally ready to date as a soldier marching to war clutching a Super Soaker.

One side of my Honda Fit was an accordion. My left shoulder throbbed as if a baby hippo sat on it.

My eyes functioned well for a ninety-five-year-old man, but I had just turned sixty-four.

I peered into my wallet, searching for the business card of a medical specialist my family doctor had recommended. Instead, I saw a single dollar bill, caught a whiff of peppermint, and heard an odd crinkly sound.

Pulling out the buck, I found the physician's business card stuck to it, along with a slightly sticky breath mint, some lint, and a condom, still in its original packaging.

Man, I thought. *What are you, George, seventeen?*

It was time to take a pit stop on my road to romance. I needed to do more than replace the mound of slag formerly known as my Honda Fit—I needed to fix me.

What woman would want a guy whose body needed a chassis realignment, new headlights, and more reliable wheels?

Exhaling slowly to center myself, I took on one challenge at a time—first the car.

A friend drove me to a lot where I haggled for a certified used 2014 Mazda3. Since it sported a stick shift, I bargained them down a thousand. It made for a great "anti-theft" device since only 18 percent of Americans can drive one.

I figured *owning* a car scored way more points than if I rolled up to a date's house in a rental, or even worse, told her I didn't have wheels and asked her to pick *me* up.

Next up? *Me.* Breathing deeply, I smiled—at least my lungs worked well. But my shoulder still hurt like hell.

My fear was that a future date would "bring me in" for a hug, then ditch me for being a cheese puff when I'd say, "No. Not on my owie."

Sorely in need of chassis realignment, I went to see a specialist in Plasma Rich Platelet (PRP) therapy. The physician used the process to treat professional hockey players who suffered muscle injuries. It got them back on their skates in days instead of weeks.

It involved drawing my blood and separating platelets from other cells. The technician used centrifugation to concentrate them.

The last step was injecting the plasma into my shoulder to speed up the healing. My insurance didn't cover the $2,000 procedure.

I signed up anyway. After my first shot, I imagined millions of microscopic Georges sporting manly khaki shorts, hard at work in my shoulder, massaging my injured muscles.

In my mind, the platelets worked to the beat of the group Queen singing, *We will, we will, rub you!*

Success! Two days after the first injection, I put more pressure on the hurt arm in bed without wincing in pain. After the second shot, my "boo-boo" was gone. Once again, I was huggable.

Next up? Fixing my headlights. For years, women gazed into my eyes, fascinated because they couldn't describe them with just one color.

Peering into my orbs, they noticed blue, with flecks of green, and brown. But with my condition, I guessed a date would now describe them as "fair, but partly cloudy."

My ophthalmologist, Doctor Jackson, said my cataracts "weren't large, but weren't small."

"I think the word you're searching for is medium," I smiled.

The surgeon explained how he would either manually cut an incision in my eyes, remove the cataract, then insert a new lens, or zap me with a laser, remove the "bad stuff," and put in the lens.

"I'm single and searching, Doc. Does Elon Musk have anything on the market to help me stare deep inside myself to improve? Something like an introspection lens?"

"I'll tell you what," said Dr. Jackson, "I'll throw in a free book on Buddhism."

Doc batted back my screwball lines like he was Pete Rose.

I ended up choosing the Saks Fifth Avenue eye treatment package over the Dollar Store option, signing up for a Toric AOL to enhance my night and distance vision. It also fixed my astigmatism.

A benefit of my "bout of" cataracts was I brought sexy back by not needing contact lenses or glasses. Look out single women! Coming soon—George Version 2.0.

Weeks after the procedure, while driving back at dusk from work, I discovered a new world.

I don't remember that no turn on red sign, I thought. My body tingled like I chugged a sixteen-ounce can of endorphins.

Gazing straight, left, and right, instead of shades of gray and fuzzy focus, colors popped. Words miraculously appeared on diamond and rectangular signs.

Future dates would no longer fear for their lives with me as I navigated highways and back roads.

While the vision improvements helped my self-confidence, my body's worn out "wheels" cried out for maintenance too.

One date laughed when she saw my bowlegs and nicknamed me "Tex."

A second woman, noticing my limp, channeled a TV show that ran until 2012.

"Would you like some Vicodin, Dr. House?"

A third date, meeting me for the first time, noticed me limping and blurted out, "Do you have an artificial leg?"

Yes, I was a wobbly-walker, but I opted for maintenance, not total wheel replacement. I dealt with my bone-on-bone knees and "tender back" by knocking off twelve pounds, starting yoga, and lifting weights.

Moderation helped too. Instead of pushing myself to walk five miles a day, I cut it back to two, and iced my knees when I got home.

To my relief, my knee and back pain became occasional mild discomfort, and knee or back surgery wasn't necessary. *That's* when I decided to up my swagger with leg renovation.

Ever since my twenties, I wore long pants to cover my stems, even during the sweaty heat of Thailand, or the walk outside and bake summers of California.

My dates wore shirts and light blouses while I wore "sauna slacks."

"It's 100° out here. Why the long pants? Did something happen to your legs in the Army? Napalm strike?"

Beach dates were out. Parents covered their toddler's eyes when I strode onto the sand with a farmer's tan torso and milk white vampire legs. My bowlegged vanilla drumsticks formed a capital "O."

Even if my stilts were tanned, I would have covered them up.

I first started sheathing them at twenty-one when I developed ultra-high-definition blue-green bulges on my right calf—varicose veins. Now the rascals popped out on both of my ghostly legs in blue, green, red, and purple.

As a former Army DJ, I chose a surgery place with good reviews and a clever advertising slogan, *You're so vein—but we can help with that.* A Carly Simon pun? Sign me up.

A nurse brought me to the doctor's office, where a svelte blonde in her 40s waited. Ever vigilant for a worthy candidate, I picked up an important detail—she didn't have a ring on her finger.

Who needs dating apps? I thought. *The doc and I would make a perfect couple. I'd complain about what hurt, and she'd get me free drugs.*

While waiting, I looked around. Displayed on her desk was a photo of Doc with two kids, and a guy who I assumed was her husband. My "date the doctor" flirt engine sputtered to a stop, as a knock interrupted my nosiness.

It was the doctor's assistant, Katy.

"Hi, let's step into the next room. I'm here to take some pictures of your legs and send them to your insurance. And, I have some more forms for you."

As I posed we chatted. Her large diamond ring doubled as kryptonite, stopping me from unleashing a "Hey, you've already met my legs, how about getting to know the rest of me?" line.

But the sparkler on her finger failed to give her total immunity from dad jokes.

"You have my permission to fax a copy to the American Association of Retired Persons Sexy Legs Edition."

"Maybe after the procedure," she chuckled.

After about a week, the good news came in. The insurance company ruled that my gams were gnarly enough that surgery was warranted, and they'd pay.

Katy told me my operation was a minor outpatient process. That surprised me. If they were taking out veins, I fully expected they'd have to send me to la-la land.

Nope. They had me lay down on a table and injected me with a local anesthesia.

Although I preferred not to be, I was wide awake.

I sensed a tug, but no pain. Then a warm spaghetti noodle splat against my cheek.

"Whoops," went the doctor.

Not what I wanted to hear. Did she sever an artery? Chop off a chunk of calf? Lose a scalpel in my thigh?

"Don't worry," said Dr. Frankenstein. "I slapped you with a bit of you—a piece of vein. It's all right. You don't need it anymore."

Now *she* was quick with the jokes. I squelched my impulse to yelp like a startled puppy.

"That's all right, Doc. I used to be in the Army. I can take it."

That, of course, was a stretch. Sure, I was in the service, but I was a broadcast journalist, not infantry. Add to that, I'd never been struck in the face with an inner part of my body.

"Sorry," she said.

"That's fine, doc. Am I beautiful yet? Do you think someone might mistake my stilts for George Clooney's?"

"Maybe," she said, adding, "if he has bowlegs."

We both laughed.

My varicose vein-free but still pale, white, crooked stems were ready for shorts, and some sun.

In a few weeks, my legs healed, and so did my self-esteem. I was old, but now my stilts looked more appealing.

Still, it wasn't quite time to unleash "the Georgester" back onto the online dating scene.

First, I needed to downsize. My son Brandon was attending the University of Santa Barbara. My daughter Shannon moved out of the house to City College in the same city.

My home in Murrieta was too big for a single gray wolf whose two cubs left the den. I needed to save some cheddar to help the kids with school costs, so I sold the house, held an estate sale, and invested the cash in their future.

That created another challenge. Sure, my body was healed, and I was ready to date again, but my new digs made it appear like I was a welfare dad looking for a sugar momma to rescue him.

In 2018, I ended up in a single-floor, two-bedroom house a fifteen-minute walk from my work. All 111 of the 1950s-era homes had sturdy, thick, dirty beige concrete walls and double-paned windows.

The adjacent military airport contributed soot and noise to the community ambiance. The houses were older than me, as were most of my neighbors.

One octogenarian with curly silver hair said "hi" when she saw me, then invited me to dinner. While flattered, I had no desire to become a boy toy for a woman my mom's age.

Despite insecurities about my home, I decided to open my heart again, and hope no one stomped on it with stilettos.

Grabbing some sparkling water, I mixed in some apple juice, and plopped on my comfy office chair. My mission? Travel through the untamed wilderness of online singles in a quest for the future Mrs. Smith.

Since I last logged on, three women messaged me: Meow Or Never, Butter Me Up, and Thanos Swiped Right.

Meow's profile indicated she liked a movie called *The Notebook*, walks, and guys who didn't play games.

Her head and shoulders photo resembled a model's out of a Vogue shoot, making me skeptical. Why was a late twenties redhead messaging a silverback like me?

My profile noted I was seeking a woman, from 45 to 64. Hers said she wanted a guy 30 to 99. The remainder of her bio was blank.

Butter either craved flattery or fantasized about lathering up like a Turkey with Land O' Lakes.

The twenty-eight-year-old woman with blonde hair liked *The Notebook*, walks, and guys who didn't play games. The rest of her life's story? Blank.

Hmm, I thought. *Maybe she's a roomie with Meow, and they've made filling out profiles a group project.*

Surely, Thanos Swiped Right would be different. She was a twenty-six-year old brunette.

With that name, her hair should at least have purple streaks. Her favorite movie? Too easy. *Avengers: Infinity War!* Right? Nope. *The Notebook* AND she liked walks and fellas who didn't play games.

It puzzled me how a fraudster who came up with three creative usernames failed to close the scam with varying bios.

The catfisher probably thought most men only paid attention to the photo and name, and considered blank spaces on the bio a red flag.

Amused, but refusing to bite, I moved on.

As I continued swiping, I stumbled on to an interesting woman in San Diego. I was about to take a business trip to her birth country.

10. Me? Oedipus?

I had just returned from a January 2018 business trip to Seoul, South Korea, when I decided to contact a woman who'd caught my eye right before I'd left.

The Korean-American woman, Lee, lived in San Diego. She looked fifty, but was seven years older.

Her headline? "Successful businesswoman searching for a like-minded man for a serious relationship or marriage."

While "serious" is a word no one uses to describe me, I shot her a message.

I said I'd just returned from the country of her birth from a business trip. *And* that in the 1970s I served as an Army broadcaster in Seoul, Taegu, Munsan, and Dongducheon—where I came to love Korean food and culture.

For bonus points, I said that I created a Black Pink playlist on Spotify and loved the song "Gangnam Style."

"Black who? Gangnam what?" she asked. My bonding attempt died there. While my music tastes resembled that of a twenty-year-old girl, hers did not.

After exchanging a few messages, we chatted on the phone. Lee spoke English with a strong accent. She was proud to have earned her American citizenship, in her words, "long ago."

We decided to meet in a Korean barbecue restaurant on the outskirts of San Diego.

"Annyeonghaseyo" (hi,) I said in Korean, using one of the twenty-five words I still remembered.

"Great," said Lee, sparing me by not launching into Korean.

I ordered a variety platter for us: bulgogi (marinated beef), short ribs, pork belly, and vegetables. The waiter served up the goodies on a dome-shaped grill in the middle of our table.

He maneuvered an exhaust fan on an accordion-like spring several inches above our roasting food to vacuum up the fumes. It spared us from leaving the restaurant later and smelling like "pork-belly-scented cologne."

Corn and cheese filled one half of the outside rim of the grill. It melted fast, forming a cheesy crust. Scrambled eggs mixed with flour filled the remaining half of the outside rim.

"This is great, George," smiled Lee. "Most first dates are sipping coffee."

"I have a confession," I said, glancing down in embarrassment at my chopsticks. "I'm an addict."

"Excuse me???"

"I can't go a month without bulgogi. It's been a month since I last scarfed it down in Seoul. I need another fix."

For added impact, I rattled my hand so the piece of meat I picked off the grill with my chopsticks fell.

She chuckled.

Lee told me she lived in the port city of Pusan (now Busan) before she immigrated to California, where she worked in personnel for a Korean company that valued her dual language skills.

Unlike some past dates she showed an active interest in me.

"What was it like living in Korea as an American DJ?"

"Well, I loved it. Koreans tuned in to our radio and TV as a gateway to uncensored news. Some learned English."

I went on to explain that in the late 1970s, twenty million locals dialed in our color TV broadcasts. Korean stations broadcast in black and white. People hungered for the American perspective at a time when President Park Chung Hee clamped a lid on any news outlet critical of his government.

"I bet the girls went crazy for you," smiled Lee. "Were you a star?"

"Fans wrote me lots of handwritten letters. A Korean pop music magazine did a feature on me."

I fished out the magazine from the backpack I carried into the restaurant to show her.

"Wow. That's more than forty years old," she said.

Turning back to our lunch, her eyes widened when she saw me spear some pungent, orange cabbage with my chopsticks.

"You like kimchi. Not everyone does. That's your second helping!"

"I learned to love it," I said. "I used to say Yaki Mandu and kimchi too, when I went into a restaurant. And I loved takuan."

"What?" she asked.

"Japanese pickled yellow radishes."

"Oh," she said, "takuan."

I swear she pronounced it the same way I did.

We lingered a full two hours in the restaurant chatting, said goodbye, and agreed to do it again.

Nice job, I told myself, replaying the day in my head as I drove home. While not a fan of the hour drive, she was worth it.

Anxious for an objective analysis of the rendezvous, I sought out my friends, Kate and Jef.

The following Monday, I joined them at a picnic table under a patio cover at the AFN Broadcast Center in Riverside.

"What if she's some kind of weirdo. Maybe she's only into me for my wrinkles?"

146

Jef laughed. Kate piled on, "Uh-huh. Dad jokes to match the dad body."

"Are you good with an hour drive?" Jef asked as he finished a burger.

"Good for now, but sure, I wish she lived closer," I replied.

Lee and I continued to chat over the next few days. The Super Bowl was coming up. I suggested we meet the weekend *after* the big game since she never watched football.

There was no way I was going to miss my team, the Philadelphia Eagles, take on the New England Patriots.

Lee insisted she didn't mind me watching the game at her house, even volunteering to cook. My job? Prep and clean up!

I was still a tad hesitant to spend the day with someone who didn't normally watch football, but on February 4, 2018, I jumped into my Mazda3 for the hour trek to her place in San Diego.

When I exited the highway and started to draw closer to her address, it seemed the only cars people owned were Teslas, Mercedes, Lexuses, and BMWs. A mansion on her street sported all four—but maybe one of them was the maid's.

When Waze signaled I had arrived, my eyes bulged. Sculpted scrubs, rugged boulders, and a mini waterfall all complemented her modern two-floor home. Her yard resembled something from landscape painter Thomas Cole.

I laughed to myself. If a buyer witnessed my parked subcompact in Lee's driveway, the asking price for her house would plummet 30K.

When I pushed the Ring button, I expected a valet to answer, give me a number, and ask for my keys. But no. It was Lee.

"Take off your shoes."

Her harsh tone, directness, and 'missing hello' threw me.

Hmmm. I thought. I cupped my hand, raised it to my nose, and inhaled. *Nope. No trace of the bean burrito with cheese I had for breakfast. Maybe it's the Mazda. I should have parked it in front of someone else's place.*

"Hi, Lee. Lovely home," I said, handing her a bouquet of roses.

"Oh, thanks," she softened. "Come in."

Her response wasn't what I expected. She reacted like she wasn't sure what to do with unsolicited vegetation.

As my eyes adjusted to the inside light, my jaw did a cartoon-like bounce off my chest. Twice.

The white marble floor glistened. Cherub statues of different sizes dotted the room. A winding staircase with a gold-colored handrail stretched heavenward to the second floor.

Feeling like a relic strolling through relics, I wondered if the art was Italian—maybe on loan from the Metropolitan Museum of Art in Naples.

As we walked into the living room, I spotted a large white leather couch about ten feet from the TV. Sweet! Soon I'd be sprawled on it watching the game.

Lee had already started meal prep. She asked me to use a step ladder to snare a vase she shoved in the back of an upper shelf. Remarkably, it was dust-free.

"I'm not a fan of cut flowers," she said. "Potted plants last much longer."

Wow. I thought. *I'm never going to have to guess what she's thinking.*

"What can I do to help?" I asked.

Lee handed me a knife. She asked me to chop up some broccoli. I went full Gordon Ramsay on the green stuff, slicing half of it up for the stir fry.

"No, no," she said, grabbing the remaining broccoli from me. While I had sliced from the florets to the stem, she cut off each broccoli top to avoid dusting the cutting board with tiny green particles.

My next three attempts to help prepare the food ended no better. With each try, Lee jumped in with tips on how to work more efficiently. Raising a white flag in my mind, I decided to change the subject.

"The personnel business has been good to you, Lee. Your house is exquisite."

"Well, the job helps, but most of my income comes from my three rental homes in Temecula. You should invest in a few."

Unbelievable! Her response to a compliment? More unsolicited commentary on how *I* could do better.

I smiled. "May I have one of yours?"

Her face remained granite. Yet another dad line sputtered and smoldered..

"Lee, the game's about to start. You're sure you're good with me morphing into a sofa sloth?"

"Yes, how long is it?"

"About three and a half hours," I said. "We can eat at halftime. That's about ninety minutes from now. Do you want to sit with me? I can explain the game."

"No," she said. "I have plenty to do. Relax. Enjoy."

I settled down on the sofa with a beer and a bag of Doritos I'd brought with me.

Oddsmakers picked the Patriots to win. Tom Brady and Rob Gronkowski deserved to be the favorites. Still, I dared hope. Eagles Quarterback Nick Foles had played well in the playoffs.

The game started close. In the second quarter, a pass from Foles bounced off a receiver, and the Pats recovered around the Eagles' three-yard line.

"Damn it!" I yelled, caught up in the game.

"Could you lower your voice?" instructed Lee from the kitchen. "And you shouldn't have your feet on the table."

Whoops. I guess I was too relaxed. I contemplated joking with her that I was buffing the wood with my stocking feet, but passed.

Right before halftime, the Eagles huddled on a fourth and two. Foles lined up in the shotgun. He moved to the right side of the offensive line.

Tight end Trey Burton tossed the ball to the quarterback for a wide-open touchdown. The team called it "The Philly Special."

"Yeeeess," I yelled.

"George!" admonished Lee once again.

"Sorry," I replied. I started to regret spending Super Bowl Sunday with a non-sports fan, even if she was lovely, and was certainly no Venmo Vixen. For all I knew, she might own Venmo.

"And oh," she added. "Why are you wearing a short-sleeved shirt? Aren't you cold?"

Man, I told myself. I selected the black dress shirt because I wanted to impress when I showed up for the date. I looked good in it. It seemed no matter how much I tried, the George machine was failing to gain any traction.

Halftime began. I sat down and joined Lee for dinner. The marinated spare ribs, rice, and broccoli rocked. The meat popped with flavor, with noticeably less salt than a restaurant's.

"Everything is delicious," I said. "Sorry if I got a bit too enthusiastic during the game."

"You *really* like football," she said, in a tone that struck me as puzzled disapproval. Right then, all of the remarks she had made since I arrived came together to form a conclusion in my brain.

"Lee, I made a mistake coming over for the Super Bowl."

"Why?"

"Well, ever since I walked in the door, I've been doing little things you disapprove of. I brought you the wrong kind of flowers, failed to slice the broccoli right, got too loud, put my feet on the table, and wore the wrong shirt."

"Oh!" she said. "That's why people call me 'mom' at work. I'm always telling them what to do."

"Lee, I already have a mom. But the job of girlfriend is open. Why don't you join me on the couch?"

"No. I'll pass. I have some paperwork to do."

I turned my thoughts back to the game. The second half went back and forth, with New England taking the lead, 33–32, in the fourth quarter.

Lee circled by, glanced my way, and reached down by my leg.

Hold on, I thought. *Is a tender caress coming my way?*

She pulled her hand up, avoiding my leg. As she raised her hand from the floor, it clenched a jagged, orange fragment of Dorito. Lee locked eyes with me, saying nothing.

"Oh, thanks," I said, plucking it from her fingers and popping it in my mouth. "I was all out."

Yup, I was making a statement.

Her face froze. While she said nothing, I imagined she was having second thoughts about opening her multimillion-dollar home to a Neanderthal driving wheels marginally classier than Fred Flintstone's log car.

Back to the game. With time running out, Foles drove the Eagles down the field, nailing a pass to Zach Ertz. He dove into the end zone for a touchdown.

"Yes," I yelled, standing up, before sitting down again. Lee glanced my way.

"You should sit up straight."

I ignored her, too absorbed in my happiness to let her comment fully enter my consciousness.

Brady started another one of his drives as my eyes focused on the action. He launched a desperation heave into the end zone for tight end Rob Gronkowski, who missed the jump ball. The Eagles won, 41–33!

"It's over?" asked Lee.

"It is. My team won. Look, I never should have come to your house to watch a football game. It didn't work out. We got on each other's nerves."

"Well, now that the game's over, would you like to stay overnight?"

"Lee, I would love that, but we're not a good match."

We went back and forth about it for a few minutes. Then I kissed her on the cheek, put my shoes on, and left.

My chance to marry a sugar momma ended on date number two. If she were telling me to sit up straight on our second date, what would she be doing if we got married? Turn to me during dinner and tell me to open my mouth, to make sure I chewed enough before swallowing?

There were other things too. The long drive to her place was exhausting. Most importantly, the spark I originally had for her had fizzled out like a two-day-old can of open Coke.

Unlike the tragic Greek Oedipus, I wasn't looking for a maternal figure. I saw myself more as Jason of the Argonauts, still sailing on, setbacks and all, in search of a new love.

If I eventually found the Golden Fleece, I'd make sweaters and matching mittens from it for two!

11. My Psychologist Is Paranoid

After fleeing from Lee, the beautiful San Diego siren, I set sail once again on my love odyssey.

It didn't take long to meet someone new. Logging on, my computer "dinged" with good news. After a two-week delay, a woman I had messaged finally responded.

Jane started out apologizing for the communication delay, explaining she was out of the country visiting her mom in Taiwan.

Over the next few weeks, we exchanged messages and photos. I liked that she was close with her family, especially her mom.

The trip she was on the previous week was a flight to Taiwan to boost her sick Mom's spirits.

We chatted and agreed to meet in a coffee shop in Rowland Heights, about an hour from me.

Several days before our rendezvous, I got a puzzling photo and message from her: the Chinese word for luck on an arm.

"It's a nice tattoo," she texted.

The only problem? I didn't have any tattoos and wasn't thinking about getting one.

She was mixing me up with another guy.

The next day, I went in for a haircut and gave my stylist a crazy request.

"Kelly, you paint landscapes on the side. How about I commission you for a five-minute art project after the trim?"

"What do you have in mind?" she asked.

"Here's the canvas," I replied, pointing to my shoulder. "And I bought the art supplies with me," handing her a black Sharpie.

That's when I opened my phone and pointed at the image of the Chinese word for luck. I told her the story.

"That's hilarious," Kelly said, "I'll do it."

Luckily for me, her next client canceled, so she had time to etch her first tattoo. I tipped her $20 for a $30 haircut and my first ever ink.

The following day I drove to meet Jane at a coffee shop near her home. She chose a quaint place tucked in the corner, removed from a mall with outdoor tables and lots of empty chairs.

What made it especially easy to spot her was she was the only person sitting outside.

My date was short—about 5-foot-3—with a nice figure and long black hair that cascaded halfway down her back. She was in her mid-fifties, but appeared more forty-something. She wore no makeup.

I guessed the only ointment she used was sunscreen to protect her fair skin.

"Hi, George," she said, rising to meet me and extending a hand, "Jane."

"What are you drinking?" I asked, smiling.

"Green tea," she said, thinking for a moment, then adding, "Oh. I forgot something, I'll be right back." With that, she hurried to a silver Toyota Camry and drove off.

What did I do wrong? I thought.

I cupped my breath and inhaled. Nope. I detected spearmint, with a hint of Cheerios. Raising my arms, I sniffed. Someone might walk by thinking I was sipping a piña colada, but it was my coconut-scented Secret deodorant.

As I vegetated with my cafe latte and glanced at Jane's cooling green tea, I thought about leaving. She said she'd be back, but what if this was her stone-cold non-confrontational way of saying I wasn't her type?

Just as I started to ponder leaving, she drove up and parked.

"I'm back," smiled Jane, shutting her car door and walking toward me, clutching a paper plate covered with aluminum foil, topped with a blue ribbon.

"This is for you for driving so far to meet me."

I was surprised, relieved, and flattered.

"I baked some peanut butter cookies," she said. "I forgot them on the counter and went back to grab them."

We settled in over my latte and her lukewarm green tea. Occasionally, cars passed by. People chatted inside the cafe. But other than that, the only voices filling the morning air were ours. We talked under our sun umbrella and relaxed.

I rolled up my sleeve and angled my shoulder toward her.

"What do you think of my tattoo?" I said as I unveiled my hairdresser's Sharpie masterpiece.

Her face morphed from confused to thoughtful to amused.

"I've seen that ink somewhere before," she smiled.

"But not on a deluxe quality canvas like this," I said, pointing at my arm.

I fished out my phone and showed her the image and her comment in our message stream.

"I didn't realize I sent that to you by mistake," Jane said, peering more closely at the Chinese word for luck on my shoulder. "Does it come off?"

Dabbing my napkin into a glass of water on our table, I rubbed the ink. A third of it came off on my napkin.

"Any more tattoos?" she asked.

Moving my hands to my belt like I was going to drop my pants for a big reveal, I stopped, chuckled, and sat down.

"Nope!"

Switching gears, she turned back to small talk.

"You have a bachelor's in Television Production and Communication?" asked Jane.

"Yup," I said. "You wrote on your profile that you have a Master's in Psychology, you're from Taiwan, and work at an import/export business. Has your education helped you with that?"

"It helps me to relate to other people. I chose it because I want to understand myself better. Eventually, I want to earn a PhD and become a practicing psychologist here in the States for Chinese Americans."

Our chat had run about an hour when I circled back inside the cafe to grab an English muffin for each of us. I wanted to save the peanut butter cookies she'd gifted me for later.

Talking with her was easy. She listened and figured out that I liked to set up jokes with straight-faced sincerity.

We hugged, and she agreed to go hiking with me the following Saturday and have lunch.

Not waiting for the weekend, we phoned every night. The hike was a blast and led to other treks.

In a month, we were hanging out at her place. When she asked me to watch her favorite show, *How to Commit Murder,* I paused, then asked why.

"If you want to get rid of an ex-boyfriend, just block him. No need for violence."

I'd never seen the show, but it sounded like an instruction manual. Hannibal Lecter was a psychiatrist, which to me, was close enough to a psychologist, just with a fancier prescription pad and a scarier dinner menu.

Adding to my touch of paranoia about her—a previous related conversation with my brother Paul.

I had an hour-long talk with him the previous month when I flew to visit my family in Pennsylvania. Like me, he was single and searching.

Paul didn't have cable, but was so addicted to *Forensic Files* that he asked permission from my mother to come over to her house in rural Pennsylvania to tune it in.

When Mom said yes, my bro went over and binged the show every day for a week.

As we sat in a bar sipping beer, I said, "Paul, it's great seeing you again, but all you're talking about is the *Forensic Files*. I hope you don't do that on your dates. You don't want them to think you're fixated on how to commit the perfect murder. How about trying Hallmark movies or PBS?"

"It's funny you mention that . . . " he said, putting down his empty glass to talk.

He was interrupted by a full-figured waitress with purple-streaked black hair, swinging by with a second round.

As she placed the beer on the table, she smiled at us. I grinned back. Paul totally missed the opportunity, lasering his eyes on me, not the sexy beer bringer.

His eyes glistened and his hand shook impatiently as he waited for the waitress to leave. Once she did, he continued.

"Like I was saying . . . in one show the woman picked up a guy from a dating site, made him dinner and drinks and took a few months to slowly poison him with arsenic."

"Why would she do that?"

"She tricked the guy into signing a life insurance policy," said Paul.

"Paul," I said, "It's becoming clear why you don't get many second dates."

While there were parallels with my brother's obsession with *Forensic Files* and Jane's fixation with *How to Commit Murder*, my brief morbid fantasy passed. After all, my girlfriend never made me sign up for life insurance. Plus, I never heard of a serial killer who was a dog lover.

Jane adored her pooches. Every day, we'd take her two fur balls, Bao and Mao Mao, for a walk, I mean roll, to a nearby park. She didn't want the dogs walking on the street or the dirt leading to the grassy part of the park. That's why I pushed them in a baby carriage.

That four-wheeler resembled a palace on wheels, with two-inch wide tires, a lacy canopy with gold accents, and an inside lined with leather.

People walked toward us with smiles. Maybe they were conditioned to grin when a baby approached. Perhaps they found it ridiculous to spend so much on a carriage, or thought it comical to witness an older couple with a newborn. My theory is that their smiling gave them an excuse to stare at us longer than is normally polite.

Whenever people approached us, I grinned back. They glanced into our four-wheeler, expecting to coo at an infant, only to discover two hairy heads, panting, with large extended tongues.

Bao and Mao Mao bobbed up and down whenever we struck a sidewalk crack. Once we rolled onto the grassy part of the park, Jane lifted the furballs out to frolic.

After about fifteen minutes, I pulled a rag that I brought with us, poured some water on it, washed the pooches' paws, and placed them back in their home on wheels.

Mao Mao was a black toy poodle mixed with a Maltese.

"Did you name him after the Great Chairman?"

"Of course not," Jane said. "I'm from Taiwan. Mao Mao means 'small child,' or 'baby.' "

"Well, Mao Mao is cute," I said. "It fits."

What puzzled me was when I researched the name on Google, I found out Mao Mao was also a pet's identifier for a cat.

Hmm, I smiled to myself. *Maybe Mao Mao was a cat currently identifying as a dog.*

Bao was a brown Maltese and Toy Poodle mix. Like her sister, she weighed about fifteen pounds.

"Bao" is soft and fluffy, like a steamed bun," said Jane. "It's often stuffed with barbecue pork."

"Ah—so it's not that your Bao has a hankering for Bao," I giggled.

Stony silence met my wit. Note to self. Don't poke fun at her fur babies. But I found it hard not to. Bao's distinguishing feature was a large bulge under its chin—the size of a Bao.

"What's that lump?" I asked.

It looked about the size of a steamed bun, but I didn't say it outloud.

"It's a tumor."

"Oh. Sorry. Will you have it taken out?"

"I'm worried the operation would kill her," said Jane. "So she'll live with it."

Sheathing my wisecracks, I reached down and petted the pooches. Jokes aside, they were affectionate, clean, and rarely barked. Good dogs.

That night, I appreciated the pooches' exceptional hygiene even more when Jane invited me to stay over.

After I pulled on my Ronald Reagan onesie, Jane shook her head without laughing. She said nothing as I slid under the covers on my side of the bed.

As my woman brushed her teeth, a scurrying sound caught my ear. Then, rustling sheets. Turning over my shoulder, I stared straight into two pairs of eyes framed with thick hair as Mao Mao and Bao joined me.

"Uh, are the hairy ones supposed to be in bed?"

"Sure! Why not?"

Dreams of a night of romance ended. As Jane turned off the lights in the bathroom, Mao Mao settled in above my head, and Bao burrowed under the sheets to curl up between my legs.

"They like you," she said, smiling as she got into bed, giving me a kiss on the cheek. "Good night!"

"I'm a bit worried I may hurt them if I roll over," I said with concern, mixed in with one last try to make the bed a humans-only zone.

"They'll move over," she said. "I'm so happy you're good with dogs."

Instead of fighting, I banked the points I'd earned, leaned over, and kissed Jane good night.

As I lay there, déjá vu kicked me in the nuts. When I was married, my former wife insisted that she bring both my kids into our "family bed" when she was nursing. Then, when "supper was over," they stayed the night.

For me, nothing popped the romance bubble faster than leaning over for affection with my spouse only to lock eyes with my child.

With those thoughts percolating in my mind as I dozed off, I dreamed.

My grown-up children, Brandon and Shannon, were lying in bed with Jane and me. Then they sat up, pointed at her, and gasped, "Who's she?"

Before I could answer, Mao Mao and Bao burst out from under the sheets and started licking my kids' feet. Brandon and Shannon grinned and started playing with them.

Then the dream morphed into a nightmare. I developed a tumor on my leg. Someone told me to ignore it. Sweating and short of breath, I woke up.

Disoriented, I opened my eyes and clutched my limb, and found a tumor—Bao's. She stirred a bit when my hand brushed against her throat, then stopped.

"Everything all right?" asked Jane, lying a few feet away.

"All's good," I replied as the pooch continued a restful sleep between my legs. "I hope Bao doesn't dream that she's hungry."

She chuckled, rolled over, and went back to bed. In a few minutes, I did too.

The next morning, I stirred and woke up. I glanced down, glimpsed Bao, and detected a pulse. Happy I hadn't crushed the critter, I rolled out of bed.

I left after we enjoyed a leisurely breakfast.

Over the following month, Jane and I continued dating, mixing in hikes, movies, and TV nights watching *How to Commit Murder*.

One day, we shared our thoughts on religion. I mentioned I grew up Methodist.

I told her a minister helped me deal with difficulties I was having with my ex-wife in Germany. And, when we divorced, another pastor, a mile from my home, John Hansen, and his church inspired me. I overcame my sadness and loneliness.

"How about you?" I asked.

"I'm a spiritualist," she said.

My body stiffened. A year ago, I dated another psychologist, Jackie, and she said the same words.

Had my once-and-done date come back again, in spirit form, trading her white woman shell for that of a petite Asian?

"I believe everyone has a spirituality," continued Jane. "We take separate trails."

"What's your path?" I asked.

"I follow some tenets of Buddhism, with my own ideas of meditation."

"Do you believe a person's spirit could be in someone, then move on into another?"

"Huh? That's crazy! Of course not."

166

Whew. I thought. It wasn't Jackie. You can never be too sure. More importantly, I wasn't ready for a relationship with someone who believes in "spirit musical chairs" and prays to Casper the friendly ghost.

"How about we go to church together?" Jane asked, stirring me from my thoughts.

I agreed, and we went. Later, when she met my mom, it sparked her interest enough that she borrowed a book discussing the nuances and beliefs of Christianity.

Soon after that, Jane and I started delving into the subject of our former partners. She shared how she hated her ex-husband and only came to his deathbed out of obligation. I talked about my kids and immediate family, but avoided talking about my former spouse.

"Why don't you talk about her?" asked Jane.

"Because my thoughts are on you, not her."

"I want you to," said my psychologist girlfriend, pausing before pivoting into an unsolicited free therapy session.

"I think you may still be in love with your ex."

"Wow. Where did that come from?" I asked. "I can't believe you'd think that. Wait until I call Brigitte tonight. She won't believe it either."

By Jane's raised eyebrows, I guessed it was the wrong time for levity.

"How can I understand you?" she asked. "You refuse to open up to me about it."

In the midst of a perfect 75° hike, I surrendered and begrudgingly shared why my ex and I divorced, concluding with:

"The door to a rekindling of romance with my ex is not only closed, it's bricked over, and dropped into shark-invested waters in the Pacific."

As we talked, the sun dimmed. The path became more treacherous. I grew thirsty. But now that I had opened up and explained my feelings, I sighed, content. It felt like someone yanked a rucksack of rocks off my back and handed me a chilled bottle of water. Now Jane and I could allow our relationship to flourish.

Relieved, I gazed deep into Jane's eyes and said, "I'm happy to be with you."

Over the coming weeks, the subject of my former wife didn't come up again. Our thoughts changed to our upcoming trip to Germany.

The American Forces Network (AFN) broadcast center in Riverside was sending me to a conference in Germany. I'd spent twenty-eight years there as a soldier and a DOD civilian, got married in Frankfurt, and my son and daughter were born there.

Jane and I agreed to take a vacation together after I wrapped up my work. She'd never visited Europe.

We agreed I'd concentrate on work, then she'd fly over to join me. After our seminar ended, we'd see Europe. My boss gave me two weeks off.

When my plane touched down in Frankfurt, I sighed happily. I was back to a place that was home.

Picking up my rental car, I zipped down the autobahn at 120 mph. I hit that speed after the airport area, because I suspected traffic cameras awaited, hidden in the shadows of an underpass.

Sure enough, ten years after I left Germany, they were still snapping shots of speeders. Three separate boxes, each with a red lens mounted on permanent poles pointed at different lanes. The Germans relied on photography, not police with radar guns. Arguing a speeding ticket is hard to do when you open an envelope to behold a letter with your face behind the wheel and your speed superimposed beneath it.

I checked into the Gasthaus (a small restaurant and hotel) where the conference was being held. That night, I sat down with Bill, a co-worker and friend.

Amidst the hum of people talking and the clinking of beer mugs, Bill and I hoisted frothy pilsners and chowed down on schnitzel (breaded pork) and potato salad.

I didn't like American taters and fixings, but drooled over the German Kartoffelsalat.

Their spuds featured vinegar instead of mayo, with other yummy ingredients like bacon and mustard.

"How's the dating life?" asked my buddy. "Did you trade your DJ hot hits for a string quartet?"

That was Bill's way of asking if I was still with Kim, the classical music concert cellist.

"Nope. I decided I wanted less music written by guys with powdered wigs. I've moved on," I said. "Now I'm seeing a woman, Jane. She's pointing out who made me into a mess. She's a psychologist."

"So who's to blame, your mom or dad?"

"Me," I smiled. "Because I don't hate my ex-wife."

"Man," he snickered, "Lucky you! Free therapy!"

"Here's something even nuttier," I said, after gulping a bit more Pilsner Urquell. "She's the second psychologist I dated. The first one lasted one date. She said spirits pass from one person to another."

"Wow," said Bill, motioning to the barkeep for another round. "Maybe the spirit of that first girlfriend wandered into the body of your current one. She's ghosting you!"

It may have been the beer, but the same thought had come into my mind. I hooted.

The next morning, before the last day of my seminar started, my ex, Brigitte, came by to pick up a boogie board she'd left behind in the

States.   Knowing Jane's predilection for paranoia, I'd let my girlfriend know in advance what I was doing.

I met Brigitte outside my hotel room and handed her the boogie board.

"Hi, George," she said. "Have a little time to talk? Can I step inside?"

"No, I wish I did—but everything starts soon," I said. "Greetings from Brandon and Shannon."

She crinkled her nose and frowned a bit. "Say hi to your husband for me," I said as I handed her the board and darted toward the conference room.

Some hours later, we wrapped up our meeting. I zipped to the lobby desk to check in on Jane's arrival. I'd set it up for the Gasthouse shuttle to pick her up at the airport.

"Has Jane Liu arrived yet?" I asked. "She was supposed to come in by now."

"She's here," said the clerk with a smile, pointing at a table thirty feet away and handing me a second room key.

"Welcome to Germany," I said with a grin, moving toward her with arms extended.

"Hi," she said with icicles dangling off each letter. "Let's go to the room."

"What's up? A problem with the shuttle?"

"No. They wouldn't give me a card to the room until you showed up at the desk. What are you hiding?

"What??"

When we arrived outside my room, Jane jammed her plastic card into the door slot, bumping me aside to go in first. She moved like an energized Viola Davis from *How to Get Away with Murder,* staring under the bed, and peering under the sheets and pillows. She opened every dresser drawer, then headed for the bathroom.

"I didn't kill anybody," I laughed. "And even if I did, I've learned enough from watching TV with you to cover my tracks."

"It isn't funny. You met your ex here. Did she stay overnight? Why do I see two bars of soap in the shower dish? What's this shirt in the closet? I don't remember you having one like that!"

I felt like I'd been transported back in time as a defendant at the Nuremberg War Trials.

"Jane, she picked up the boogie board and didn't come in. My virtue is intact."

"Jokes. Always jokes."

I took a slow breath and exhaled slowly before answering.

"I don't think anything I say is making a difference," I sighed. "If you don't trust me, I'll pay for another shuttle and you can fly back home."

That helped. She stopped her frenzied search for traces of female DNA.

"Okay. It's been a long flight," she said. "I'm stressed. I'm sorry. Let's start over."

We went on a stroll around the Gasthaus and relaxed with afternoon tea and some pastry. The next day, I packed up our stuff and we drove off for Heidelberg.

I was excited to show Jane around. After strolling through the old town's cobblestone streets, we headed to the castle. As we walked hand-in-hand, I mentioned one of my favorite writers, Mark Twain, who spent time in the city in 1878.

He, too, found it beautiful and romantic, writing *A Tramp Abroad*.

I'd already visited Heidelberg six or seven times before when I lived in Germany, but always enjoyed its musky old walls and scenic overlook of the Neckar River. Like me, Jane drank in the history of the place, stopping to read about the castle, built in 1214.

"In comparison, the United States is a toddler," I said.

Everything appeared smooth with us. But, as often happens, I was wrong.

The next day, we went on a trip to the town where I lived during my last eight years in Germany: Leistadt, a suburb of Bad Dürkheim. The town is home to the "Wurstmarkt."

Yeah, it sounds like "worst market," but it's not.

Every September, citizens gear up for the biggest Wine festival in Germany. I don't understand why they don't call it that. Sure, they have "wursts" (sausages), but people come for the vino!

My former house in Germany was nestled several hundred yards from vineyards in a quiet cul-de-sac on top of a hill. Every year, the people on our street gathered for a neighborhood party.

Every week, I'd send Shannon out to knock on doors and give them some of my home-baked peanut butter cookies, orange danish, and brownies. They thought I was a master baker. Little did they know my secret was opening a box or pouch of mix from the U.S. commissary, adding water and egg and shoving it in the oven.

One neighborhood grandma didn't like sweets. In her case, I'd stroll by, knock, then sit outside her house on an outdoor bench with her, sipping wine.

Even though I'd been in the States for seven years, I'd kept in touch. A few German couples visited my family in California.

Now, a local news bulletin swept the cul-de-sac. George was back after his divorce with a new love.

Friends Matthias and Marion set up an outdoor dinner at their place and invited folks to swing by. I wasn't sure how many people would come, but fifteen did.

Bottles of locally produced Dornfelders, Rieslings, and Spatburgunders dotted the table, along with overflowing wooden plates of cheese and fruit. And that was just the beginning! Spargelcremesuppe (white asparagus with cream) came out. Then, Flammkuchen, a type of thin crust pizza topped with crème fraîche bacon, and onions.

Fortunately, one of my former neighbors offered us a room to stay after the party. I introduced Jane and told everyone how we met. People asked her questions about her import/export business and what she thought of Germany. The cul-de-sac tales began to flow as freely as the wine.

"We miss the Berg (town) Gorilla," chuckled Klemens.

Once during Fasching (carnival), I dressed up in an ape suit. Daughter Shannon accompanied me, wearing a Pippi Longstocking costume.

"My friend would like a banana," my mini-me asked the grandma who answered the door.

"What?"

That's when I came from around the corner with my hand outstretched, making "ouu ouu ouu" sounds.

"Ahhh," screamed the old lady. Thankfully, her heart held out. She whacked me hard on the head.

"George!" She yelled, somehow knowing it was me, not my teenage son or wife.

We howled.

As the stories from years past ended, my thoughts returned to the present.

"Bitte, noch eine glass (please another)," I said to Frank, the man next to me, as I motioned for more Dornfelder. It's a smooth, dry, red wine.

"It's probably a coincidence," said my former neighbor Kristin, "But ever since you left, Helga's flat iron art has remained naked!"

I leaned over to explain to Jane that I used to sneak out at night and dress the modern rusty metal silhouette of a person in a straw hat, Hawaiian shirt, or bikini—whatever spares lay around the house.

After about thirty minutes of light conversation and many laughs, a friendly lady from the end of the cul-de-sac, Bettina, said something that made me choke on my Flammkuchen.

"Brigitte was wonderful for our street too; she's a great friend."

Why is she mentioning her? I thought. *She's not here. I don't understand it.*

My pleasant wine buzz began to flicker out.

"How is she doing?" asked Bettina.

"I have no idea," I said, glancing over at Jane, who sat staring at the German woman.

Flushing red and uncomfortable, I tried to change the subject, but my former neighbor kept talking about my former wife.

Finally, another neighbor spoke up, asking me if I'd found any good California wines.

"Not yet," I said, relieved, he extricated me from a tar pit I'd been unable to pry myself from on my own.

In time, the relaxed, jovial atmosphere returned. Ninety minutes later, the party broke up. I thanked everyone for coming. That night, as Jane and I curled up to go to bed, she brought up the conversation with Bettina.

"You should have said you're happy to be with me and didn't want to talk about Brigitte."

"Jane, I'm divorced, and I am here with you," I said. "But you're right. It's my mistake. I should have spoken up. I'm sorry."

I meant it. The wine wasn't a good excuse. As the sun's rays snuck into the house, I thanked Matthias and Marion for their hospitality, gathered up our luggage, and headed out in our rental car for Frankfurt.

That night in our hotel in Frankfurt, around three in the morning, Jane got a phone call and jumped out of bed. She tiptoed into the bathroom, shutting it quietly behind her. There was no way I could sleep after that. I lay there, listening to hushed words. I couldn't understand a word. It was all in Mandarin.

My girlfriend spent an hour, before emerging with misty eyes and a downturned face.

"What's going on?" I asked.

"It's my mom," Jane replied. "She's sick. She needs me and my sisters to come to her."

"Is she dying?"

"No. But she goes through times like this where she's sad. She asks the family to come to her. When I moved to the States, I promised her I'd be a plane flight away. I must go."

She opened her purse and produced six $100 bills.

"I won't be able to go with you to Croatia, I have to book a flight to Taiwan. So I'm going to reimburse you."

Jane seemed more concerned and embarrassed about me paying for a plane ticket she wasn't going to use than the health of her mom.

"You don't have to do that," I said.

"No, I insist," she said.

"Let me earn it," I smiled, thinking of a way to lighten the mood. I started dancing in my Sloth pajamas. Edging closer to her, I gazed into her eyes.

"Tip?"

She giggled, shook her head, and one by one, tipped me six times.

Since we were awake anyway, we packed up. I drove to the airport and returned the rental car.

We hugged and parted inside the terminal. I walked to the gate to prepare to board my plane to Croatia. She peeled off for the China Airlines flight bound for Taiwan to visit her mom.

Dubrovnik was everything I hoped for. Many *Game of Thrones* scenes were shot in the city by the Adriatic Sea.

I took a day tour, posing where Cersei Lannister stumbled down stairs on her walk of shame, where she chose the Mountain as her champion, and where some of the battle of Blackwater Bay took place.

It hit me then that single life wasn't so bad. I was having a blast without Jane. Increasingly, when we talked, I worried she was diagnosing me mid-sentence. Sometimes she made me feel more like a patient than a boyfriend.

July 2018 was an exciting time to visit. The country of less than four million was full of pride. Everywhere I went, flags of red, white, and blue with a centered Croatian coat of arms fluttered in the breeze.

The small nation's soccer team was making a deep run into the World Cup.

Around me, banners flew, and scores of TVs of every size were set up for people to check out the home team taking on favored England.

Grabbing a table for one in the town square, I relished the experience. Laughing to myself, I thought if Jane happened to unexpectedly show up, she'd see me sitting alone at a table for four and accuse me of holding a seat vacant in case my ex showed up.

As I sipped beer, waiting for the match to begin, I pondered the timing of that phone call the night we were scheduled to fly to Croatia.

Was Jane's mother sick, or was she looking for an excuse to bail?

It was then that my imagination kicked in—fueled by the pitcher of beer and the walking tour I had of "King's Landing" sites of *Game of Thrones*.

Hearing a man and a woman arguing I turned my head to see a beautiful blonde woman arguing with a taxi driver over surge prices.

It was Daenerys Targaryen, the Mother of Dragons. Croatia had instituted a no-fly zone because of the World Cup.

She pulled up a chair, and sat down beside me.

"I heard your girlfriend abandoned you. I never would. Stay at my side. We will rule the Seven Kingdoms."

Before my shock could wear off, Melisandre, the Red Woman sorceress, glided up, wearing a full length crimson dress that sparkled supernaturally under the Dubrovnik evening lights.

"She's lying," she purred. "When someone else comes along, she'll Dracarys you into a

flaming shish-kabob. With me, you'll live forever."

Recovering a bit, and flattered to have two gorgeous women fighting to date me, I spoke up.

"That sounds great, but I always confuse your name with Missandei. May I call you Betty?"

Right on cue Missandei, the beautiful former slave girl translator, rode up on a scooter.

"You can call me whatever you like, George, just don't call me late to bed. Grey Worm is a skilled warrior with a big heart, but he's still a eunuch. I want to get caught up on lost snuggle time."

Just as the trio started tugging on me, cheering shattered my imaginary moment.

The stunning women faded into smoky wisps.

The cheers came from the old town Dubrovnik crowd. Croatia won!

Mario Mandzukic, a player I'd followed and admired when he played for my favorite team, Bayern Munich, scored the winning goal in extra time.

People roared. Friends clunked beer glasses. Teenagers ran by holding Croatian flags.

Days later, I returned to the same plaza to watch Croatia take on France in the World Cup final.

Sadly, the French won 4 to 2.

While Mandzukic scored a late goal, he also messed up and put France on the board first with an "own goal."

I flew out of Croatia the next day for home, looking forward to the coming week.

Jane was arriving at LAX from Taiwan, and my daughter Shannon was flying back from Germany at about the same time. My girlfriend picked up my daughter and they drove to my place. It was the first time they met.

The meeting turned out to be a consequential one.

The two of them chatted for about two hours in the car, with Jane, true to her psychologist roots, asking lots of questions.

Shannon put in a good word for me, telling Jane how she enjoyed spending time with me.

My daughter talked about my love of current and classic music, mixing my Spotify playlists with equal doses of new Selena Gomez and Taylor Swift, and old tunes from the Rolling Stones.

She complimented Jane, saying how great it was that she was in my life.

When they rolled up to my house, I greeted both with hugs. My girlfriend and I peeled off for the master bedroom, while Shannon crashed in the adjacent room.

The next morning, my therapist—I mean girlfriend—rose at five. She said she had to leave.

"What's up?" I asked.

"Nothing. Enjoy time with your daughter," she said.

"You can stay too," I replied. "Shannon enjoys your company."

Jane half-turned, shook her head no, grabbed her purse, and left. I followed her out and waved. She didn't glance back.

Something was off. She seemed cold. Aloof. After mulling it over, I called, and it went right to voice mail.

"Jane, call me," I texted.

I forgot my concerns as I turned to housework and made some pancakes for Shannon. Two hours later, I got a text from Jane.

"George, your daughter still needs you. You're not ready for a relationship with me. Please don't call back."

What!!! I thought. *This is insane. First, I can't get over my former wife, and now this? Worst of all, she didn't have the courage to talk to me about it face-to-face.*

All my thoughts and experiences coalesced. Jane hated her ex-husband and remained convinced I should react the same way toward my former spouse. I wholeheartedly disagreed.

When Brigitte and I ended our marriage, any romantic feelings we once shared ended. What remained was a shared commitment to doing what's best for our children.

With her living in Germany and me in the States, long distance communication was a whole lot easier to do when we maintained a respectful, cooperative relationship.

Jane, on the other hand, lived a tepid, non-emotional existence with her son. She parented as a Tiger Mom, pushing him to achieve the highest grades, and become a doctor, or better yet, a physician on weekdays, and a lawyer on the weekends.

She had no patience or time for bonding, humor, or fun. She thought my personal connection with Shannon should be just like she had with her son

My psychologist needed a shrink. I think she majored in psychology to better understand herself.

Me? I wanted a new partner to love and cherish, as my number one–but without relegating my kids, siblings, and mother to a constant "waiting on deck" status.

In retrospect, my time with Jane felt more like she was quizzing and studying me for a future doctoral dissertation than dating me.

Honestly, I would have been much better off living in my head with the beauties from *Game of Thrones*—and, unbeknownst to all of us, they'd have been much better off with me.

The following year, in 2019, in the final season of the series, they'd all meet a tragic end.

My search had gone on for three years. If it went on much longer, and I found someone, we'd need his and hers walkers.

It seemed more and more likely I would spend my final days with fellow silver hairs yelling out "Bingo," and "Yahtzee."

12. An Accountant Doesn't Add Up

In 2019, I considered swapping Match and Zoosk for the Meetup app.

That way I could spend the rest of my life with fellow board gamers battling it out with *Axis and Allies*, or *Settlers of Catan*.

While optimistic by nature, I had to face reality. I had moved out of the 55 to 64 age bracket. Dating apps use ranges to help with matching and filtering.

When I updated my profile to show I turned sixty-five in 2019, I thought my computer took a power hit and froze the screen. My average of ten weekly messages plunged to zero.

Even the scammers stopped writing.

It was right around then that a former Army buddy of mine reached out to get together.

It was midday on a Wednesday, and we'd scored an outside table under blue skies, palm trees, and 73° weather. We got caught up over plates of Mexican food and some margaritas.

"How's the dating life going?" asked my friend, Perry. He and his wife Jean met me for lunch at the Mission Inn in Riverside,

California, a historic one-block building modeled after a Spanish mission.

"Well, my 'best by' date expired," I said. "They're searching for someone younger."

Then I told some of my dating stories, including the psychologist trying to treat me, the "perfume bandit" trying to rip me off, and the Thai trying to seduce me for a green card.

"Man," laughed Perry. "You should write a book!"

(And so I did).

"You're not giving up, are you?" asked Jean.

"Well, I'm afraid right now if I meet a bachelorette in person, she's likely to tell me, 'Aw, you're funny. My *dad* would love you!' "

We laughed and swapped updates on our kids. I shared that Brandon and Shannon were out of the house and attending college in Santa Barbara.

After dessert and a coffee, we said our farewells. That talk with Jean and Perry helped re-energize me to get back into online dating.

Maybe I just needed to vent a bit. I jumped back with both sky-blue Crocs into the dating pool.

About a week later, a woman snagged my attention, Lisa. She lived thirty minutes away, sported a slender build, and had short black hair mixed with dark brown highlights. She went to college in Beijing. Her hobby? Travel.

I shot her a note.

The next day, a return message came.

We exchanged a few texts, then I called her. Since we both worked, we decided to meet the following Saturday. The rendezvous place of choice?

Yes. I'm predictable. Starbucks.

When I walked in the door, I recognized her and smiled. She glanced my way and smiled back. Walking over, I shook her hand and grabbed a latte and breakfast sandwich for both of us.

"Props to you on working as an accountant," I said. "Math and I broke up in high school. It was a toxic relationship."

She laughed.

"Come on, you're not that bad."

"I eked out a D- in high school algebra in eleventh grade and retook it in summer school to avoid flunking out."

"But didn't you say you went to college?" she asked.

Oops. I thought. Time to shift out of the self-deprecating humor and balance my image. If not, she'll think I was lying about my degree, or, instead of studying, spent my childhood snacking on lead paint.

"I did well at my university," I said. "I got a Bachelor of Arts and graduated with honors in the top 10 percent of my class."

Seeing the lingering disbelief in her eyes, I continued.

"In my defense, not knowing what 3x-2 x y+c meant hasn't hurt me. But I wish I had paid attention in high school German. I saw no practical need for it. Then the Army sent me to Europe and I married a German!"

"What changed you from a poor student into a good one?" asked Lisa.

"Money, time, and attitude. I started Ohio University at the age of twenty-seven because I wanted to earn a degree to up my credentials and return to Germany as a DOD civilian broadcast journalist. And since I paid for it with my savings and the GI Bill, it motivated me to study."

She smiled, relieved. If I managed to earn a university diploma, my IQ must score higher than soap.

As we sat, a group of about fifteen teenage girls came in wearing soccer jerseys. An older woman wearing khaki shorts and Nike sneakers accompanied them. By the whoops and high-fives, I assumed they won their match.

The din overpowered my conversation with Lisa. I motioned my thumb over my shoulder in the direction of the door. She smiled and nodded.

We got up and headed out. If my ears could speak, they would have thanked me for leaving and lowering my odds of needing a hearing aid later.

Outside the cafe, my date made no diversion to Nordstrom's to request pricy perfume. For the next hour, we strolled around the outdoor mall chatting.

The weather was perfect for a stroll—it felt like the mid-seventies with no humidity. Another plus? Southern California is relatively bug-free.

As we passed by families and other couples having their own talks, Lisa shared that she lived in a condo she bought in a nearby gated community.

"I live in a gated community too," I replied, "but I rent."

My inner voice whacked me, saying:

What were you going to say next, that the Air Force built it in the 1950s, and a buddy said it resembled a section eight complex?

Midway through our walk, Lisa paused and glanced at my leg.

"You've got a fast pace. I'm glad."

"Surprised?"

"Well, yes. When you walked into the coffee shop, you limped."

"Ah," I said, recognition seeping in. "I have favored my left knee ever since surgery for a torn meniscus and cartilage damage. I was bouncing my then nine-year-old daughter on my shoulders when something popped."

Lisa nodded, looking at me. She seemed to be evaluating what I said.

It was like she went to a stable to buy a horse. While it appeared I didn't need to be shot *yet*, I think she was considering moving on to another stallion.

Pausing, I thought about it, then added, "But that surgery was years ago. It doesn't stop me from afternoon walks or weekend hikes."

"That's one of my favorite hobbies," she said. "Let's go on one next week. I want to take you on a remote trail near here."

Agreeing, we met for date two. The hike went well. My knees held up.

In the months to come, we drove to the Grand Canyon, hiked the slot canyons in Utah, and toured Mexico City and the Mayan pyramids in Tulum.

When I say "we drove," to be more accurate, "she drove."

She insisted on driving her Lexus, which was bigger and newer than my Mazda—and wouldn't let me get behind the wheel, even when she started to nod off.

"Lisa," I said, "If you're going to insist on driving when you're tired, can we at least pull over first for a minute?"

"Why?"

"The swaying car is making it too hard for me to write my Last Will and Testament."

Getting my point, she pulled into a rest stop and slept for thirty minutes. Still, other than that disagreement, our relationship grew.

Three times a week, we met at her place. Her condo was tucked into a vibrant, scenic middle-class community with its own lake.

Meet at my place? Nope. Most of my neighbors were retirees, coyotes, and gophers.

Our routine was after work, I drove over to her home for dinner, then we strolled by the lake.

One night, Lisa told me about an upcoming community event she wanted to attend. It was when the HOA stocked the pond with fish.

The following Saturday, the trout barely had time to "unpack" before Lisa pulled two fishing poles from storage and suggested we welcome them—to her frying pan.

My problem? The only thing I knew about the fish was don't overcook them. My sole certainty about fishing was if you wanted to catch one, a pole was a solid choice.

"Don't worry, George," said my girlfriend. "Let's just have fun!"

Strolling out to the lake, I noticed fishermen spaced out about every twenty feet around the thirty acre lake.

It was a community blowout. Everywhere I looked, families in lawn chairs laughed with their kids and chowed down on picnic lunches.

"I got one!" yelled a boy who looked about ten to an adult I assumed was his dad.

He started reeling it in as Papa thrust out a net to snare the critter.

Well, if he can do it, I can, I told myself. (Not because I *believed* what I was saying—I just wanted to boost my self-confidence.)

Lisa and I were by the water for about twenty minutes when my fishing pole dipped and the line went taut.

"It's Moby Dick's baby brother—Mini Dick!" I yelled.

"Pull it in, George!" said Lisa.

Then, a few feet away from shore, my reel jammed.

I turned, looking for a stone or stick to toss at the trout to stun it. Finding none, I slowly started walking backward, thinking I could drag it out of the water.

"Hold still," instructed a stranger, moving fast past me with a net as he waded into the lake in his wading boots.

He scooped up the trout, came back to us, and dumped it into the cooler Lisa brought with us.

"It's a beaut," said the man. "Looks about five pounds!"

Then the fisherman samaritan took time to examine my pole to see what went wrong.

"You've got a real bird's nest there!"

"'I don't know about that," I replied, "But it sure is a tangled mess!"

While my new fisherman friend, Jake, worked on my fishing line, Lisa yelled with excitement. Her pole was bobbing up and down.

After a battle that was much shorter than mine, and with none of the drama, she reeled in a fine finned fellow who looked like my catch's cousin.

Jake put down my now untangled fishing pole, stuck out his net, snared Lisa's catch from the lake, and dumped it into our cooler.

We thanked him and headed back to the apartment for dinner.

That evening my girlfriend scaled, gutted, and cooked the fish, serving them up with some rice and steamed broccoli.

I was ready to take our relationship to the next level.

For younger couples, the major moment of reckoning comes when your partner meets your parents. For me, the big moment came when I introduced her to my son Brandon, and his girlfriend, Idalia.

We'd decided to meet halfway between their apartment in Santa Barbara and Lisa's place. Since my son preferred greens to enter his body in a second-hand kind of way, we met at a steakhouse.

"Lisa, meet Brandon and Idalia," I said as we met in the parking lot outside of the restaurant. The aroma of roasting beef greeted us as we mosied in.

Chatting as we walked to our table, I grinned, noticing the ease with which everyone interacted.

Lisa shared what life was like in 1989 Beijing when she was a college student.

"I was one of the protestors at Tiananmen Square in June of 1989."

Right then the food arrived.

Brandon showed remarkable willpower, asking a follow-on question instead of digging into his steak.

"Wow. What was that like?"

"It was crazy. The square became a city in a city. Thousands of students put up tents and lived there for days, calling for more freedom."

"Tell them what happened to you," I said. (She'd told me the story before.)

"A family friend told me soldiers would be coming and told me not to be there. The day before the tanks came I left. I'm lucky I did. Hundreds were killed. Some of my friends were hurt or arrested and they made a list of everyone who was at the square."

"So they still let you leave China for the States?" asked Brandon.

"Yes, a few years later they did, but they never would have let me go if I would have been on that list. I was very lucky."

As we dug into the food, talk changed to a lighter subject.

"So how did you meet?" asked Idalia.

Lisa turned her head to me. I answered.

"On a dating app. Zoosk!"

My face involuntarily reddened when I said it. When I first ventured into the wilds of online dating, I felt embarrassed that I was doing it.

Before I started swiping, the only rendezvous app I'd ever heard of was Tinder—which I thought was for people with strong libidos in search of one-night "wham, bam, thank you ma'am (or sir)" hookups.

Even after a few years of online dating, a little of that stigma stuck in my brain. Part of me felt saying I met my girlfriend online was an admission that I failed in meeting a woman the "normal" way, through family and friends, or at church, work, or a club.

Keep in mind that when I dated in the 1970s, Al Gore hadn't yet invented the internet. (I'm joking. I know he didn't. Elon Musk did.)

Guilt lingered without reason.

Pulling my thoughts back to my "introduce my girlfriend to my son meeting," I ordered a monster brownie for the four of us to split. It was then that Lisa opened her purse and gave Brandon and Idalia a small gift bag.

"Wow, that's so nice," said Idalia with a grin.

Brandon reached inside and pulled out two small decorative bowls and an Apple Music gift card. I smiled at Lisa's thoughtful gesture.

The dinner was a great success.

A few weeks later, Lisa brought me to her company's Christmas party. She had no immediate family. Her parents had passed, and she had no kids. I slipped on a Hugo Boss suit, red silk tie, and white shirt to impress.

Throughout the night, I shook hands, told entertaining stories, and never once dribbled sauce on myself.

Once, when I went to the bar to grab drinks for us, I turned, catching Lisa chatting with Helen, her best friend at work. They smiled my way.

As we drove home, I turned to Lisa, ready to bask in second-hand compliments about her witty, dashing boyfriend.

"Did Helen say what she thinks of me?"

"She said you're nice, but old."

"Are you sure, she said, 'old?' Maybe she said, 'funny?' "

"No. Funny doesn't sound at all like old. She said, 'old.' "

Failing in my fishing, I tweaked my question.

"Well, how about you? You don't think I'm a prune, do you?"

"You're an attractive man, but you have a turkey neck. It shows your age."

Ouch. A slow hiss cut through the silence in the car—the sound of my ego deflating. Yes, the folds under my chin resembled a gobbler's, but I thought no one noticed them except me.

"Okay, not what I expected, but I did ask," I said.

Settling into my "I am who I am" mode, I reentered a state of blissfully ignoring my flaws. But then Lisa reminded me. And reminded me again.

Take the time when I sat watching TV while she gazed at me instead of *Star Trek: Picard*.

"If you move your chin up and hold it taut for a few minutes every day, you'll tighten your neck muscles."

"Lisa, don't you think Jean-Luc is more interesting than the folds of my neck? He's trying to save the galaxy!"

Like a mongoose biting down on a cobra, she wouldn't let go.

"Have you tried putting egg whites on at night?"

"All that will do is make my neck shiny. I am not a loaf of baking bread!"

Noting my irritation, she stopped.

Still, it was clear her friend's comment about my skin folds stuck. Now my relationship with her focused on the part of my body located between my shoulders and jaw.

I became self-conscious about my neck, holding my chin up for pictures to lengthen my muscles and reduce the jowls.

Now, when she watched me, I thought she was looking at me not with love, but with the critical eye of a home remedy specialist, positive she could help, if I'd only listen.

Long neck stretches and egg whites didn't help, so I decided to regain my swagger with the help of a nip and tuck doctor.

He told me a lower facelift would give me the throat of a thirty-year-old. The doctor showed me before-and-after pictures. His flawless, svelte assistant jumped in to say she had the same procedure, pointing to her neck.

Sold!

"While you're at it, would you like me to fix those eyebags of yours?" asked the surgeon.

"What eyebags?" I joked.

But I was aware of them. For fifteen years, co-workers in Germany, including one commander, continually asked if I was tired.

Nope. It was the layers of skin and dark circles plopped under my peepers.

"How does it work?" I asked.

"I'll take some fat from your belly and inject it a few inches under your eyes. The process smooths out those bags and reinvigorates you. You'll look years younger."

"Go for it doc. Purge my flaws and release the sexy beast."

Walking out to the lobby, I sat down to watch the rotating before and after photos on a wall-sized screen. All of the newly renovated people were women. The three people in the waiting room were all women.

"So do many guys come in for face lifts?" I asked.

"We have men come in for Botox all the time," she said.

She still hadn't answered my question.

"How about facelifts?"

"Not as many," she smiled. "You'll be an influencer!"

"I'd rather not," I said with a serious face. "I'm hiding from an ex-girlfriend who made me go to bed dressed up like Kermit the Frog and call her Miss Piggy."

The receptionist chuckled in a "It's not funny, but you're the customer, so I'll laugh" kind of way.

A month later, in November 2019, Lisa took a few hours off, drove me to my appointment, and waited for me.

A few hours later, I emerged with my head wrapped like a mummy. A tube dangled from behind each ear, leading to a small plastic drainage bottle. A nurse wheeled me out on a wheelchair to Lisa. I greeted her.

"Mom! What are you doing here?"

Lisa seemed irritated by my humor and turned to the nurse. I expected her to ask something about my care, but she asked something else.

"Do you have some plastic for the seat? I don't want him to leak in my car."

Hmm. I thought to myself. She's no Mother Teresa.

My nurse raised her eyebrows, said "Hold on a moment," and returned a few minutes later with a large piece of plastic.

Once Lisa pulled her car up front, the nurse helped her put it over the back seat. Then the caregiver helped me back into the vehicle.

My girlfriend had previously made it clear she wasn't going to help me. Fortunately, my friends Lu Harrington and Larry Sichter said they would.

My "no way in hell am I a Florence Nightingale" drove me to their house. My buddies met me at the car and navigated me into their guest bedroom.

I appreciated having good friends. Lisa appreciated not having to keep her engine running for too long while I stumbled out of the car.

In a week, I circled back to my plastic surgeon to get my bandages taken off and the stitches removed.

My face looked like I lost "Fight Club," then got run over by a minivan. Still, it didn't stop me from going to work the following week.

Co-workers stared. I came up with a different explanation each time someone was bold enough to ask me what happened.

"It's not my dominatrix's fault. I forgot the safe word."

"I'm transitioning to Ryan Reynolds."

"Never, ever order the Puffer Fish sushi."

Lisa took her time seeing me again. She said she wanted me to heal and not rush it, but I suspected she didn't want to see a face that looked like a half done road construction project.

Sure, I'm damaged goods, I thought, *but it was her comments about my gobbler neck that sparked my decision to get the surgery. That's why my face looks like Mr. Potato Head's!*

When I finally got my girlfriend's permission to swing by, my reflection still said "yikes," but I thirsted for encouragement.

"Remember me?" I asked. "What do you think?"

Swiveling my head left, right, up, and down, I froze like a posing model and smiled seductively.

Lisa stared, but not at my neck.

"You have a red dot on both sides of your face where they injected fat under your eyes."

"Oh," I said. "I'm sure it will fade."

Flushed, I walked inside, self-conscious instead of encouraged. We ate dinner and got caught up. She suggested we pass on our usual stroll around the lake.

"Let's forget the walk tonight. I don't think the breeze will help you heal. Rest will."

Over the coming weeks, Lisa focused more on the red dots on my face than on my wrinkle-free neck.

"The dots haven't gone away!"

"I know," I said, irritated. "Are you suggesting I pay for more plastic surgery to fix the plastic surgery?"

"No. I'm saying you have two red pin marks on your face."

Other oddities popped up. While she lay down in bed, I gave her a back rub. In mid-knead, Lisa leaned over, grabbed her phone, and began scrolling.

"Aren't you enjoying this?"

"*You* wanted to give me one," she replied, "I thought it was something *you* liked."

I stopped.

"Lisa, something's on your mind," I said. "Wanna talk about it?"

"I'm glad you asked," she said. "You've mentioned before that you plan to buy a house sometime, right?"

"Yes, I have the money in the bank. When the time's right, I'll buy a place and we can move in together. Your place would make a great rental."

"How about this?" she said. "You buy a house near here and live in it, and I live here?"

"That's strange. Why wouldn't we live together?"

She didn't answer me.

"Lisa, before I buy a house, we should spend more time together. We're only visiting each other three days a week."

She paused, exhaled, and said, "I think it's better if we make it two days a week. I've decided I'm going to quit my job and study for the rest of the year so I can pass the Certified Public Accountant test. I need to focus."

"I understand," I said, "I support you taking a major step to boost your career. Let me think about all this."

We hugged, and I left.

As I drove home, disappointment and frustration set in.

Lisa needed a friendly neighbor, not a husband. Why else would she ask me to buy a house near her, but not live together?

Once I pulled up at my place, I called back. We chatted and agreed to go our separate ways.

Unbeknownst to us, a microscopic critter would have soon broken us up anyway.

After the call to Lisa, I phoned Shannon at her off-campus apartment in Santa Barbara.

She told me the best medicine was pausing the swiping and taking some rejuvenating Daddy/Daughter time.

Both of us were no longer in a dating relationship.

The only question? Where to go?

13. I Mask to Impress

In January 2020, my then twenty-one -year-old daughter and I were both in between relationships AND wondering how a killer virus from China would impact us.

A responsible dad would have called his child to suggest she hunker down, wash her hands, and wear a mask. I didn't.

"Hey, Shannon, how about a road trip to Tijuana?"

"What!!!??"

"It's a two-for-one. We can drink to forget and build up our immunity."

"Huh!!?"

"They're calling it the Coronavirus. I'm thinking if we go to Mexico and chug Coronas, we'll strengthen our bodies against the bug."

She laughed.

"I'm down, Dad," she said, "but I'm more of a margarita girl."

"Great," I said. "Why don't you come down from Santa Barbara? I'll drive us to San Diego, then park the Mazda. We can take a streetcar to the border and foot it into Tijuana."

The following Saturday, Shannon arrived at my place in Riverside, California, about ninety minutes from downtown San Diego.

We grabbed the Blue Line to the San Ysidro station, got off, showed our passports, and started to walk to the tourist part of Tijuana.

Vendors lined both sides of the sidewalk as we walked, selling everything from candy to souvenirs.

One local wanted to sell me a donkey. Either that, or have my photo taken with the critter. I'm still not sure. My Spanish sucks.

Ahead of us, a line of taxis waited, but we blazed on.

"Let's follow the arch," I said.

I'd been to "TJ" twice before, using a large white arch as a beacon, as well as the signs pointing downtown.

When we came to a pharmacy, I asked Shannon to wait outside while I zipped in to make a purchase.

I was too embarrassed to tell her I went into the store to buy a few boxes of Mexican-produced Viagra because it was one-fifth of the cost in the States.

While I wasn't in a relationship at the moment, I wanted to be ready if a woman grabbed me and demanded, "Love me now—or in an hour when the pill kicks in."

(It wasn't until later that my friend Jef told me that sometimes Tijuana medications had fentanyl or amphetamines in them, or no active ingredient.)

Shannon and I walked over a bridge above the highway along the border and peered out at lines of cars and trucks snarled and stopped.

Vendors snaked their way through traffic hawking cheap trinkets, drinks, and snacks.

"I understand why you didn't want to drive, Dad."

After about twenty minutes of walking by erectile dysfunction stores, pubs, and dentist offices, we came to the base of the almost two-hundred-foot arch.

We hung a left.

Once we hit an area with lots of restaurants, a woman caught my eye with a sign, "Two beers for $3."

We went up two flights of stairs to begin "immunizing" our bodies in an outdoor restaurant.

As I drank my two Coronas and Shannon enjoyed her duet of margaritas, we toasted our single status, rejoicing that we now had more time for each other.

"SCREW DATING APPS!" we yelled, clinking our glasses.

We ordered a plate of fish tacos, along with chips and guacamole, too.

"How serious do you think this virus is going to be?" she asked.

"I'm hearing they don't understand much about it and don't have a vaccine," I replied. "No cases in the States yet, but I bet it's coming."

"Nothing we can do, except have another round," Shannon chuckled.

As we sipped and glanced over the restaurant's wooden rail to the street below, a light breeze cooled us. The scent of grilled meat wafted our way, either from the restaurant or a vendor below.

Glancing down at tourists, I saw a bunch wearing sombreros and "I ♥ Tijuana" T-shirts, while young people strolled holding hands.

"I've read that the bug dies in the heat. I hope people can still walk around like that when it hits the States," I said.

"Me too," replied Shannon. "But right now I think it's a lousy time to meet someone new. I'm not going to date for a while."

"Same here. I'll pass on sharing Corona with a stranger—the bug, or the beer."

Smiling and happy, we wrapped up our father-daughter adventure and walked back across the border.

Back home, my "drink beer and laugh about the virus" attitude gradually changed. When cases surged in March, I panicked.

I found out that old white guys like me were more at risk. Even my platelets were plotting against me! I read a study saying people with "A positive" type blood often suffered more severe reactions to the virus.

At work, my paranoia peaked. Every person not wearing a face covering was a potential germ sprayer.

Every time someone coughed, I feared the spewer was crop-dusting the room with deadly biological agents.

Some weeks after the virus arrived at my workplace, I was grateful my boss, Mike Drumheller, sent most of us home to telework.

But eventually, months of living alone in my two-bedroom house began to wear on me.

Bambi was the first to make me aware of my erratic behavior.

"George, when are you going to shave?"

"I don't have to, I'm working at home."

"Do it for me!"

"Wait a minute. *Who* are you?"

"Bambi, your girlfriend. We met on Match. We live together."

The only problem? She wasn't real. Shannon left a stuffed toy sloth at my place. I amused myself by having conversations with it and pretending I met her online.

While lonely, I had lost the desire to go back online for a real woman. Continue searching for love? How? I couldn't face the attractive lady delivering my groceries from Ralph's.

Ring, Ring.

I peeked through the peephole and yelled, "Thank you, Maria!" without opening the door. The fortyish Latina woman came by once a week, never wearing a mask. I remained inside, wearing an N95, separated from her by a thick wooden door.

Once she stepped off my porch with her coal-black mid-length hair swaying, I stepped outside wearing plastic gloves and waved at her as she drove off.

Picking up the bags, I brought them into my sunroom, sprayed each with Lysol, and waited fifteen minutes before opening the bags to put away my groceries.

As is often the case with me, my fertile imagination had evolved the pandemic into a worst-case scenario. The virus was going to kill more people than the Black Death, Spanish Flu, and Smallpox epidemics combined.

Back in 2020, I felt if there was a bright side to the pandemic, it was well hidden behind the storm.

In retrospect, I wish I could have been more like my sister, Tammy. She saw it for what it was: dangerous, but also an opportunity.

Case-in-point. I thought COVID-19 would destroy the cruise ship industry. She saw it as a wonderful opportunity to buy stocks.

Back then Royal Caribbean was selling for a low of around $19 a share. In 2025 it hit $366 a share. If I'd listened to my sister, I wouldn't still be driving a 2014 Mazda3.

Binging TV news amplified my paranoia.

One reporter from a local TV station stood interviewing students on a pier. None of them wore masks. They were defiant about it.

"Aren't you afraid of getting the virus?"

"Hell no," said one guy, with a starter mustache. "I'm young, healthy, and outside."

"What if you catch something and bring it back to class or your grandparents?"

"That's their problem. I want to live life, not hide at home like a boomer."

"Earlier I heard you joking with friends about what you call COVID," continued the blonde female reporter with blue fabric on a string covering one of her nostrils.

"Care to repeat that?" she said as the cameraman zoomed out to reveal two more students, a guy and a woman, wearing shorts and sandals.

"What do we call COVID? Boomer remover." They howled in unison.

Great. The seed was planted. Now I imagined thousands of copycat teenagers resentful of the lockdown, waiting to ambush seniors with a sneeze.

Living alone, ingesting talking head news services, wore on me. The more I watched, the more depressed I became.

Over time, I came to understand part of what those frustrated teenagers said. What kind of life was it staying cocooned inside my one-story fortress?

Shutting my government laptop, I stared at the cement wall. My eyes focused on a picture I'd hung from 1975.

I sported jungle fatigues accessorized by a huge smile.

Ah. Back then, I was happy.

I served as a DJ, slip-cueing vinyl records at U-Tapao Air Base with the American Forces Thailand Network.

My mind replaced the dismal present with me sipping on a coconut through a straw, lounging on the beach in Pattaya, and admiring scores of beautiful women in Bangkok.

But I craved new experiences, not just living vicariously in the past.

Workplace phone calls and video conferences were no substitute for real one-on-one human companionship.

I missed someone curling up with me at night and sharing a passionate morning kiss.

My loneliness battled my paranoia. I wanted to meet someone, but I was scared.

One day in March, Shannon visited me, drop-kicking away my loneliness. It was spectacular.

But a few days later, she went back to Santa Barbara, called, and gave me a scare.

"Dad, I got COVID."

"Whaaaat?"

"Don't worry," she said. "I think I caught it when I drove over to my friend before I visited you. I stayed overnight, and she was sniffling and coughing."

"What are you going to do?"

"I'm heading up to the mountain with my boyfriend and his dog. We've got a tent and we're going to camp until I'm better."

"What if your symptoms become worse?"

"Dad, we'll be fine. I'm young, tough, and buff."

Snagging one of my six COVID test kits from the kitchen drawer, I poked the Q-tip in my nose, dipped it into the kit, and waited.

My heart chugged. My sphincter tightened. I was gonna die. My synapses fired paranoid commands.

Before I croaked, I needed to clear my "sexy toes" browsing history and trash those vintage *Playboys* from the bookshelf.

Once the magazines were gone, I could fill the vacant gap with a set of *Cure Procrastination* self-help books. They were packed in a box under my bed, but I never read them.

After fifteen minutes, my "when am I going to go full-time horizontal?" paranoia ended. I gazed at the control line, with no test line.

What? I thought. *Negative?*

Refusing to believe the results, I Q-tipped my schnoz again. Negative. In two days, the same results. I didn't have COVID.

In some twisted way, I felt disappointed.

It wasn't lost on me that Shannon and I started the year in Tijuana, toasting about not dating, but now she had a boyfriend.

Yes, she caught COVID, but so what? She grabbed life by its Patagonia ski jacket and drove to a mountaintop to wait for her symptoms to pass with her BOYFRIEND!

One night, despite my fears and a six-month absence from dating, I turned on my computer, rewrote my profile, and dove back in searching for estrogen.

My new username? HealthyNoDebt.

It wasn't funny, but squished together two of my major selling points. I even added a photo of me modeling a non-kinky mask—an N95.

When I left my cement fortress, I felt a bit like Rick of *The Walking Dead*, cautious but confident, as I reconnoitered some possible sites to meet a date.

My first stop was my former favorite rendezvous spot.

Starbucks displayed a sign outside: "Drive-thru or pickup with mask only."

I slipped on my N95, ordered a Grande Latte on my app, and walked in.

The bouquet of brewing coffee remained the same, but that was about it.

Gone were the tables and chairs populated by people milking a drink for free WiFi.

Three people stood on a green one-foot-diameter dot, with six feet of distance between each other.

The usual five baristas were down to one. He stood behind a wall of plexiglass.

As I stood like an obedient soldier, I *imagined* meeting someone there for the first time.

"Hi, it's hard to tell with our masks on, but are you the woman from Zoosk? I'm George."

"Hi George, let's keep the distance for now. Did you bring your COVID test results? Are they negative?"

"Yup, here you go," I'd say, flashing my card as she flashed hers.

The barista broke up the meeting in my mind. Wanting him to hear me, I lowered my N95 off my mouth.

"Sir," he said, "If you want your drink, you'll need to keep your mask on."

Well. Starbucks was out.

My favorite restaurant, a Thai place, "Rice and Spice," offered the same sterile environment and no chance to chat.

Both choices were no-gos: order ahead and pick it up or have the food delivered.

Dating app conversations went in a new direction, too.

Before COVID, I was worried about sharing romance with a woman who might pass on the "intimacy gift that kept on giving."

Now I was more worried about "safe breathing."

I wanted a woman who believed in the merits of covering your face. Double masking was an added plus.

Someone sporting an N95 draped over a mask with insertable carbon filters was a rare gem, a keeper.

The following evening, I smiled. Three return messages waited.

One woman said COVID was a hoax, but aliens living in the ocean were real. I passed.

A second person said my overreaction to COVID indicated I'd lost something precious during the pandemic—my balls.

"What are you scared of? Waiting until they give the all clear to start living?"

"I want to lessen the odds of getting the virus now," I said. "I'm holding on for the vaccine."

"I don't believe in masks or vaccines," she replied.

And, swipe left. You're out of there! Next!

The third woman, Vivian, lived fifteen minutes from me. She discovered a positive side to the pandemic.

"I'm working from home now, and I'm happy," she said. "I rarely see others, except for my nineteen-year-old daughter. She lives with me."

We chatted on the phone and agreed to rendezvous outdoors at a park, reducing the chances of a bug sending me to the VIP room in heaven.

The date with Vivian was about to change my life.

14. COVID Flag: She Took My Breath Away

When I met Vivan at a park near her house in Riverside, California, I was more puckered up than a frat boy taking a dare to chug pickle juice.

While excited to meet her, I worried that a gang of microbes might have hitched a ride with her.

I got out of my car and walked over to her, wearing my N95. She carried one of those flimsy free hospital masks in her hand.

As I greeted her, each of my syllables was muffled by the fabric on my face.

She laughed.

"I think you said you're George. I'm Vivian. I don't think we need our masks outside, but if it makes you more comfortable, I'll wear one."

"You don't have to," I said, struggling with my inside voice, which was telling me I just invited the Grim Reaper along for our stroll.

We started walking, Vivian clutching her blue fabric, me masked and keeping a bit of distance.

When people drew close, I moved off the sidewalk onto the grass to let them pass. Some wore masks, some had none. Others adjusted their covering to protect their chin from chafing.

Vivian's next words almost made me swallow my mask.

"What attracted me to your profile is that you don't have any debt," she said. "How much do you earn a year?"

My mind rewound to earlier "I think I like you, you smell like money" first dates, like the woman who wanted me to buy her coffee and Chanel.

"Wow, you don't waste any time talking about the weather!" I said.

The crafted web of synthetic polymer fibers on my face hid my smile. It wasn't a happy grin. It was something I involuntarily broke into when thrust into an awkward situation.

I told her my salary, then asked, "Is that enough?"

She laughed. "I'm not searching for a 'Riverside Bezos,' just a guy who earns more than me. It shows you work hard."

"Ah, you're not seeking Sir Spends a Lot?" I said, relieved. "That's great. I'm not searching for a Countess of Coin."

She grinned. "Your name could be Mr. Jokes A Lot."

That made me smile and relax. I yanked off my N95 and shoved it in my pocket.

"You're getting braver, George."

"Leaving my house felt like abandoning my fortress to walk among the zombies," I said. "But the isolation was killing me faster than COVID. Talking to you is worth the risk."

Vivian's life story impressed me so much I momentarily forgot we were strolling through an outdoor petri dish.

She was born in Shanghai, became a medical doctor in the '90s, but quit for a surprising reason.

When she lived in China, international travel agents earned more than doctors, so she made a career change to become one.

It paid off. Working with high-level businessmen and government officials taught her the intricacies of how she could legally immigrate to the United States to become a citizen.

I was so engrossed in her story that I almost tripped over a soccer ball that rolled up and banged into my shin.

"Sorry," said a kid with a running water faucet of a nose, and an Adam's apple protected by a mask.

Ignoring the chubby sneeze cannon, I returned my focus to my date. She shared that she couldn't practice medicine when she came to America. She got married, had a daughter, and then in her forties, started a new career.

"I got my Master's, then a Doctor's degree in the States as an Occupational

Therapist," she said. "I work for a school district."

"Well," I said, bumping her fist to minimize germs, "We're both government employees—you county, and me federal."

The more we chatted, the more I focused on her, ignoring the mask-free germ incubators strolling past holding hands, walking their dog, or pushing a baby carriage.

I hoped Vivian was enjoying the conversation as much as I was and saw beyond my sexy exterior to the great personality underneath.

It seemed to be working. We walked around the park three times, chatting and grinning for about an hour.

The sound of our footsteps on the pavement mingled with the kids' laughing as they played.

Whiffs of two types of grass floated our way: wet lawn clippings AND pot.

Good. I thought, tapping my nose. *The honker still works. I don't have COVID. Yet.*

I turned my attention to the svelte brunette walking with me. Vivian was fourteen years younger. It wasn't an issue for either of us.

At one point, I wondered if she was taking me out on an extended walk test drive to make sure my heart didn't sputter and stop. I didn't blame her.

My body had its share of repairs, but my bowlegs, heart, and lungs still puttered along well enough to complete the hike.

At the parking lot, we called a wrap on our first rendezvous.

"Here's mine," I said, gesturing to my Mazda3.

Pausing, I volunteered to escort her to her car. She smiled and agreed.

We walked for a few minutes, stopping by her wheels. As I gazed, I pointed out we had yet another thing in common.

"What?"

"They're both white," I said. "Yours looks classier, though. What is it?"

"It's a Tesla."

She was polite, but to me, her tone told it all. I imagined her thinking:

"Nice guy, but occasionally lapses into cluelessness."

To me, a vehicle existed to transport people to places, that's it. Often, the only way I could tell one from another was if I examined the chassis and it spelled out "B-M-W" or "J-E-E-P."

Yes, it was 2020, and I couldn't recognize the bestselling car in the state of California, but in my defense—all right. I admit it. There was no excuse.

Driving home, I replayed the date. Barring that one flub, I thought I did fine. I liked Vivian and wanted to co-star with her in

Episode Two of "George Ignores COVID and Gets a Life."

A few days later, I invited her over to my *historic* Green Acres community.

When I first moved in, I believed the city called it that as an excuse to not fix the streets or renovate the houses.

But I researched it further and found out that WWII Aviator Jimmy Doolittle used to live in one of the homes, and the community's 111 buildings were listed in the National Register of Historic Places.

As we walked, that's how I sold the drab, concrete one-story house to Vivian. She smiled politely, recognizing my lame marketing ploy.

But when I told her how much I spent on rent, THAT'S when she expressed admiration.

"You're renting a two-bedroom home with a sunroom for about $1,000 less than just about anywhere in Riverside," she said.

"And that includes water, gas, and a stand-alone garage," I added.

That exchange gave me insight into her personality. Bargains impressed. Flashy exteriors, titles, and designer clothes didn't.

As we strolled through my community, we spied a bushy-tailed black and white cat nibbling on some brown nuggets on the steps to a house up ahead.

When we neared, it scurried under a parked car, and we got a better look as it ran.

That was no kitty. It was a skunk.

Later, as we walked along the fence separating private houses from March Air Reserve Base, we witnessed a family of five raccoons, unfazed by our presence and matching our pace.

"This is like a zoo," laughed Vivian.

"It's true. People don't roam much here. I notice way more wild critters than dogs. The community charges a lot for having one at your home, and you can only keep it inside. Management never erected fences between houses, so owners can't leave their pooch outside because of it."

We talked a bit more, then I brought her back to the house and cooked dinner.

Over the coming months, we strolled, talked, ate, and swung back and forth between my place and hers.

Eventually, we took another step in getting to know each other: merging our "workplaces." Sometimes I brought my laptop to her place, and other times she carried hers to Green Acres.

My pandemic fears eased, as did my loneliness. Since neither one of us went to work, I felt safer.

The only "x" factor was her then nineteen-year-old daughter, Allie, who lived with her.

She mingled with fellow students, which increased the odds of COVID hitching a ride home with her and testing the strength of my immune system.

But Vivian's daughter lanced my angst with her selflessness. She passed up her slot in a Moderna experimental serum study for me.

I drove an hour to San Diego and volunteered my body for science. They gave me cash for mileage.

"You've got a fifty-fifty chance of getting the vaccine," the needle stabber told me, aiming the syringe in the air while examining it for air bubbles.

I thought, *Wouldn't it be ironic if I came in seeking a way to keep COVID away, I thought and died from a little air in the wrong place at the wrong time?*

"I realize this is a blind test," I said, "but if you have a choice of zapping me full of antibodies, go for it!"

"Can't do that."

"That's fine. Whether it's the sweet science smoothie or a placebo, I love the prick of the needle and the soothing cool rush."

"Your behavior is a bit unusual," said the jabber, re-examining my paperwork. "Did you fill this out honestly? You said you don't do drugs, right?"

Driving back to Riverside, I rubbed my shoulder. It was either sore or wishful thinking.

Still, I smiled. I prayed that microscopic warriors patrolled my bloodstream, ready to attack and destroy invading germs.

That shot shored up my courage. I hoped it would give me a VIP pass to the outside world.

Then, Vivian tested my bravery.

"Let's go to Cancun," she suggested.

When she made the suggestion in September 2020, COVID was "going viral" across the world. The FDA had still not approved a vaccine.

I had no way of knowing if what coursed through my veins was protection, salt water, or Mountain Dew.

As a former DJ, I responded to my girlfriend with song lyrics.

"I MIGHT have been injected with go back to normal-ish serum, but in the words of Molly Hatchet, *'We're* flirting with disaster.'"

"Molly who? Is she someone you used to date?"

"Never mind that," I said. "I just think we're being reckless."

"Why?" she asked. "We don't have underlying conditions, and we'll be outside. Everyone wears masks on the plane. Plus, you might have the vaccine!"

As Vivian continued, my brain whispered to stop disagreeing and sound retreat.

"Let's invite Allie and Shannon to come," she said. "They're young and strong. They need to live life and have some fun."

I said "yes," agreeing it would be a great chance for my daughter and Vivian's to bond.

The other reason I said "yes" was I didn't want our differences on the pandemic to fracture our relationship.

When the time came for us to board our flight from LA to Cancun, I was thankful everyone wore face coverings.

Still, every time someone coughed, cleared their throat, or sniffled, my first thought was "I'm going to die."

While I felt like a guy walking into a lion's cage wearing a zebra suit, Allie was the Yin to my Yang.

Everywhere we toured in Cancun, I shielded my respiratory system with an N95 and avoided people. Not so with her.

Allie rebelled, refusing to don a face covering. She coiled like a rusty bedspring, primed to jab any fool who dared call her out for non-compliance.

When the four of us approached a narrow street leading to popular tourist restaurants, bars, and souvenir shops, I observed a man at a checkpoint. Below him was a sign in Spanish and English: MASK REQUIRED.

"Allie," I said, muffled a bit through my face covering, "If you want to follow us in, you're going to have to put on your mask."

"Screw that," she yelled, and sprinted ahead—hair flying behind her like a gazelle's tail—determined to enter on her terms.

"No," said the burly man, moving in front of her to block the way. "Mask!"

She argued for a few minutes, as a line of tourists formed behind us.

I turned the color of a strawberry margarita.

Vivian tried to reason with her.

"Sweetheart, if you want to join us, wear it. If not, we'll meet you back here in an hour."

Allie huffed, swore, and begrudgingly fished the blue fabric out of her pocket and put it on.

All four of us walked in together. The scent of roasting pork and the sound of clinking beer glasses drifted our way.

The next several days were crammed with swimming, snorkeling, tacos, and beer, until we flew home.

When we returned to California, I discovered Allie's fight to keep her face mask free was just beginning. My daughter went full Karen on people who told her to don a face covering.

Part of me understood. She couldn't take her frustration out on a virus, but could on people.

She felt masks, isolation, and shutdowns were "overkill" for young people. Shutting down public places benefited people with high cholesterol and gray hair, not her.

Worst of all for me, my paranoia about the disease put my relationship with Vivian at risk. She wanted to travel and live life. I was scared to try.

After years of "flame-out" dating experiences, I was falling in love with my girlfriend, but I needed something to shore up my courage.

Hurry up, immunizations!

Once the FDA approved the Moderna COVID-19 vaccine, I called my trial administrator, Sean, and asked him what the research team jabbed me with.

"Do I have the placebo, or the freedom fluid?" I asked.

"Welcome back from Mexico," he said, not answering my question. "I'll tell you once you come down to the clinic."

I told Sean before our vacation where I was going. While he didn't say it, I'm guessing he was pleased I mingled with lots of strangers. If I had the antibodies, it would be a good vaccine effectiveness test.

That Thursday, as I drove to San Diego, I smiled like a kid wondering if Santa delivered what he wished for.

One way or another, I told myself, *a silent warrior would be on patrol in my bloodstream.*

When I arrived, the receptionist gave me a few forms to sign, then escorted me to one of the waiting rooms.

Knock, Knock.

Sean entered with a smile.

"Congrats," he said. "You already have the vaccine."

"I thought I might," I said. "My shoulder got sore after each of my shots, and I developed a low fever."

"Yup. Typical side effects. Say. I never asked you, George. What motivated you to volunteer for the trial?"

I told him that while friends messaged me on social media complimenting me for taking a risk for humanity, that wasn't it.

The truth was, I just wanted to get back to living a normal life as fast as I could. I missed the days of going to a movie theater when the only health risk was the saturated fat in my popcorn, not the guy sitting behind me sneezing.

To some, my clinical trial made me a celebrity.

"This can't be right," said one senior official on a cruise line. A lower staffer had handed him my card because she didn't believe the date.

"They didn't start doing vaccinations in September of 2020. The FDA didn't approve it until December."

"Yes, unless you were in a clinical trial."

"You're the first I've met," he said. "Thank you for your service."

Civilians threw the same greeting my way when I was in the Army. This was the first time someone said it when all I did was volunteer because I wanted to go to the front of the line for the vaccine.

Life and love in the COVID era turned positive for me now that Vivian was in my life. Our telework "offices" merged. When we had simultaneous video meetings or phone calls, we split up and went to different rooms.

On weekends and holidays, we broke out of our isolation and traveled.

We hiked in Utah, checked out shows in Las Vegas, and visited California's Huntington Botanical Gardens.

I introduced my girlfriend to her first jet ski experience. It happened in Santa Barbara while we were visiting Brandon and Shannon.

Vivian and I had our differences, but we both worked on them. When it came to handyman abilities, I could hammer a nail correctly 50 percent of the time.

"Are you good with any tools?" asked Vivian.

"Oh yes," I replied. "My credit card."

You would think a former soldier like me would excel with cleanliness and orderliness, but that wasn't the case.

In U-Tapao, Thailand, I paid a local woman three bucks a month to make my bed, starch and press my uniforms, and polish my boots.

In Korea, while working for the U.S. military radio and TV network from 1976 to 79, I employed a house boy, a then acceptable term for the thirty-some-year-old man who did everything the Thai woman did, but for the "exorbitant" monthly rate of $20.

When I went to the NCO academy, a different houseboy prepared my wall locker and dress uniform for display. I brought an *extra* set for him that he used only for inspections.

When a drill instructor announced an upcoming wall locker inspection, I stuffed all my dirty clothes in a laundry bag, gave them to Mr. Kim, and replaced the brand-new items.

The Korean's attention to detail wowed me.

My socks, T-shirts, and underwear were tightly rolled and evenly spaced. My dress uniform had my ribbons, marksmanship badge, and collar brass aligned.

The hospital corners on my bed were so tight and neat, I side-armed a quarter at it and it skipped off the taut blanket onto the floor.

The only loose link in the equation was me. I flew through the first inspection with no gigs. Then came the second one. The inspector snapped me to attention.

"Smith!! What's up with your hygiene? Do you ever change your underwear and socks?"

"I do, drill sergeant."

"Then why do they all have a layer of dust?"

Shit. By the time I got my drawer back from Mr. Kim for the second inspection, a topping of gray dust had formed on my stuff. I neglected to shake everything off.

While I passed, he gave me two demerits.

When I left the Army as a single guy, my most valuable cleaning tool was my nose. A sniff here and a sniff there told me which socks and shirts tossed on my bed were marginally adequate to wear again.

Vivian was my polar opposite. She snagged dust particles in the air before they hit the ground.

She spaced her dresses a half-inch apart and arranged them from pure white to gray to black. Pinks led to shades of red.

I've never met a person who cared for and maintained clothes more than her.

"That's a gorgeous outfit, baby."

"Oh, this? I brought it with me from Shanghai (she left China in 1995)."

"That silver jacket is classy!"

"Glad you like it. I got it when Allie was born (the dress was nineteen years old)."

236

Just like with the armistice that ended the Korean War, my girlfriend and I established a DMZ—right there in the bathroom.

On her side, the South Korea sink and cabinet: modern, spotless, and organized.

To the "north," my territory. A casual inspector might declare my sink neat and tidy. But open the drawer and you'd uncover my hidden armaments: crammed in toothpaste tubes, shaving supplies, hair dye, and an alarming assortment of fingernail and toenail clippers.

Vivian never looked in the drawer. Peace reigned.

When it came to "clean and orderly," Vivian deserved a medal—not me. But those qualities only partially defined her.

"Baby, are you sure you're not part Sioux?"

"What?"

"They are native Americans who hunted buffalo for thousands of years in the States," I said. "Sioux ate the meat, made clothes from the hides, weapons from bones, and glue from hooves. They even treated and sewed bladders to carry water."

"What are you talking about? I'm 100 percent Chinese."

"It's because you use every part of everything."

"When construction workers throw cinder blocks and wood scraps in the dumpster, you have me dive in for them so we can build planters and garden tables. You save leftovers for compost, old clothing for rags, and coffee grounds for fertilizer."

Vivian even reused old prescription bottles.

When I opened up one pill bottle on her spice shelf, I discovered some kind of stuff that smelled like black Twizzlers. It was anise. Another time I searched for salt. I thought I found it in an old Smucker's jar, but, nope, it was sugar. I whined.

"But I labeled it," Vivian said.

"Yes," I said, pulling the container out of the cupboard and showing it to her. "But it didn't help!"

"Oh," she said, glancing at the word she scribbled on the label: 盐.

She added English names to the bottles to help me out.

My Mandarin sucked. No matter what I tried to say, my Chinese came out sounding like straining gears, not words.

I struggled so badly with her first name, "Yu," that she told me to stick with Vivian. The four Mandarin tones made my synapses spark, sputter, and short.

I believed my failure to master tones was no big thing until my girlfriend gave an example of how the wrong one changed a word's meaning.

"I'll show you what I mean," she said. "Count to five in my language."

"Yi, er, san, si . . . "

"You want to die?

"What? I didn't even make it to five!"

"The tone you used with 'si' means 'death,' not four."

"Ah," I said as my eyebrows arched. "That's why four is an unlucky number in China!"

Sometimes Vivian mispronounced English words, but it didn't bother me. After all, she did a hell of a lot better with my language than I did with hers.

Her flubs made me laugh.

Once on a ship to Alaska, she came running over to me while we were on the top deck.

"George, George," she gushed. "Humping Whales!"

"Whale sex! Wow. Where?"

"No, no, humping whales, humping whales!"

A couple walked past us laughing, moving fast in the direction Vivian was pointing.

She stood watching several breaching HUMPBACKS and wanted me to come see them.

Another time, she was waiting in the airport departure lounge with her daughter when Vivian said,

"Allie, I want crack."

"What?"

"I want crack," getting agitated and speaking louder. "CRACK, CRACK, CRACK. I want crack!"

All around them, people turned to stare.

"Mom," said Allie, whispering. "Keep the noise down. What do you want?"

"Crack," said Vivian, in a softer voice. "I'm hungry."

"Oh," said Allie, "You mean *crack-ers*," as she opened her backpack, fished out a pack of saltines, and handed them to her mom.

There were more. Vivian shocked me one night when she looked outside and said, "I really like the torture in our back yard."

While shocked she'd say that kind of thing, I gave her the benefit of the doubt. It was around Halloween at the time, and I thought maybe some kids had set up a display with the Stephen King creature Pennywise or the Demogorgon from *Stranger Things* toying with kids before dining.

Maybe she admired their creativity.

"I don't see anything out there," I said, straining my eyes in the dark.

"There, there," she exclaimed, pointing.

What she was saying was that she really liked the *torches* in our back yard! My sister

240

Lorri had gifted us a set of solar lights that flickered like they had flames inside.

My friend Tony also has a Chinese wife. I shared Vivian's word flubs with him, wondering if he could relate.

He tilted his head back and roared.

"I'll say. Last week, we were sitting on the couch, relaxing, and she turned to me and said, 'I like toe sucking!' "

"Really, baby?" he asked. "I thought you wanted to chill tonight with TV?"

"What did she mean?" I asked Tony.

"She was saying she enjoyed the Sylvester Stallone TV show, *Tulsa King.*

My friend and I agreed. Moments like that ushered in added sparks of joy to our relationships.

That was just one way Vivian brought spice to my life. She was the "pao" in my Kung Pao Chicken.

We shared a love of travel, wanted to be with each other, but gave each other space, overlooked each other's flaws, and had an eye for no one but each other.

Yes, (cue the violins and falling rose petals) we found love.

On Valentine's Day, 2021, I proposed, and she said yes. When I told family and friends, they reacted with a mix of happiness, surprise, and relief.

"I'm happy for you, Dad," said Brandon, adding, "And for us too. Now someone else is in your life to play Settlers of Catan with you. Not just us."

"The old dinosaur is making a comeback," laughed my buddy Steve.

"She sits up straight. I like that," said my mom.

"What is that, fifty dates in five years?" asked my friend Roy over the phone. "Your slutting days are over."

I laughed. He didn't know, he was just poking me.

Later, when I added up the different women I met once and done for coffee, and those I had a more serious relationship with, the total was close to thirty. My journey to meet my new wife was a long one, but worth it.

In March, in the middle of the great germ apocalypse, we started planning our wedding. Vivian's first marriage was a small ceremony at the courthouse, with no pageantry.

"I've always dreamed of walking down the church aisle wearing a beautiful white dress," Vivian said.

"What a coincidence," I replied, "Me too!"

"Be serious!"

Wanting to live, I reeled in the humor.

Her brother, who still lived in China, sent her a gorgeous ivory gown with a flowing train. The bare-armed, low back masterpiece wowed like something you'd see on the Hallmark Movie Channel.

Next up, we searched for a venue, which wasn't easy in the days of COVID. Some were closed. Others restricted how many could attend.

We locked in "Thee Olde Wedding Chapel" in Riverside. Throwing in those extra "e's" made the joint sound extra classy.

Seriously, we agreed it was perfect.

The church featured hardwood floors, with thirty rows of stained oak pews. The center aisle was just the right size to allow a beautiful bride to complete her bridal walk to the altar to the admiration of all.

Two days before our ceremony, Vivian and I went on an early morning walk in my secluded, gated community.

What was different? My soon-to-be wife carried a pair of garden clippers clutched in one hand. She held a large plastic garbage bag with the other.

"Are you sure you want to do this?" I asked.

"Of course, why should we pay when I can do it for free?"

The word "free" never failed to bring a grin to Vivian's face. Her pulse raced, she grew short of breath, and her face flushed.

We kept strolling. No one walked the streets. Perhaps because of COVID. Maybe because most of the residents were older and preferred to stay inside to avoid blisters and chafing.

The only life we encountered were crows, sparrows, and ground squirrels. We stopped.

"Hold these," she said, snipping some flowers from the community property.

A few minutes later, we paused again. "Here you go," she said, pruning some wild, green ferns and handing them to me.

Next up, we walked down another street. A patch of pale, yellow roses appeared.

Clip, clip, clip went Vivian's snippers.

"That should be enough," she said.

Once back home, she went to work with a pile of lace, green accents, and fasteners she'd bought months before online.

In just two days, she built a stunning floral centerpiece for the altar and vibrant natural flower accents for each pew seat lining the center aisle of the church.

A professional florist couldn't have done a better job—and would have charged ten times more.

The day before the ceremony, Brandon and his girlfriend Idalia came down to our place. Shannon and her boyfriend Nolan came as well.

That evening, we sat down to enjoy some gin and tonics, a few bottles of cabernet, and assorted chunks of cheese. After several hours, inspiration lit up my eyes.

"Brandon, let's take this party on the road and hit some bars."

"Dad, we already did, don't you remember?"

"Huh?"

"Look. You're sixty-eight. You forget stuff. How could you not remember when you got up on stage to dance with those overweight male strippers wearing 'I heart seniors' underpants and N95 face masks?"

"Huh?"

"As your best man, it's my responsibility to guarantee we're all at the church tomorrow, not waking up in a suite with Mike Tyson's tigers. Besides, you're paranoid about COVID. Do you really want to go to a bar?"

Brandon was right. Instead, we downed a few gin and tonics at my house, and called it a night.

Since the wedding was during the pandemic, it was a small one—just fourteen people. I didn't want my mom, brothers, and sisters, or Vivian's parents to fly out and risk their health.

The ceremony blended my wife's eye for beauty with my goofball antics. It started with a memorable flower boy: twenty-something Nolan.

He pirouetted down the middle of the church, throwing some of the rose petals Vivian had harvested two days prior.

Next, Idalia played the iconic "Here Comes The Bride" on my portable boombox. Vivian walked down the aisle, her childhood dream realized, with Allie and Shannon holding her bridal train.

She stopped at the altar, where Larry Sichter, a good friend I worked with in Germany and California, awaited.

Up until our big day, my buddy hadn't been to a religious site since he went to a black evangelical church to research a play he was in. His dark Catholic shirt with a white collar came from the same show.

He became a reverend courtesy of the internet and $30.

"Do you take this man to be your husband, and trust him to guard you and the infinity stones from Ultron, till death do you part?" asked the reverend, as Allie handed Vivian a gold ring adorned with six stones for my hand."

"I do."

"And do you, George," continued Larry, "Promise to value and cherish Vivian, as you now present her with the largest rock in the state?"

That's when Brandon passed me a monster two-inch plastic "diamond" that lit up when it touched her finger.

"I do."

We kissed and hugged, then mugged for photos.

With COVID restricting the number of people attending, I roped everyone into servitude.

I asked all the guests to stick around after the event to sweep up rose petals and take down the floral decorations before the next party arrived.

Buddy Roy Mason brought a portable margarita bar in his car's trunk. We all downed them before entering the reception restaurant, the Big Sky Bistro, our favorite Chinese eatery in Riverside, California.

All fourteen of us pulled up for a sumptuous dinner at a huge rotating glass table. We filled up with lobster, tofu, honeyed shrimp with walnuts, bok choy, steamed pork buns, and egg tarts.

As I sipped on a Tsingtao beer, I pondered the long journey that led me to the moment I now enjoyed.

When the coronavirus first reared its microscopic head, I joked about it in Tijuana while drinking bottles of brew with the same name.

Later, the bug paralyzed me into avoiding people, especially dates. But Vivian encouraged me to leave my Korean War era concrete house and live life.

When I think back to the pandemic, I laugh at myself and see the irony in what unfolded. My search for love ended six years later with a COVID-era marriage.

Someday, when I have grandkids, I look forward to telling them pandemic stories.

"What did you do during the germ apocalypse, Grandpa?"

"I got married!

15. Swiped Out

My quest for love came to an end before my knees or back did. Southern California Starbucks and discount gas station sales slumped. Relieved, I sanded down the callus on my swiping finger.

A sixty-something single dad found love online, overcoming creaky bones, a pancaked car, and "seductive fundraisers."

Pondering my more than six-year quest, I made mistakes, learned a lot, and with help along the way, persevered.

From the beginning, family and friends reminded me to be cautious. No woman was going to ride up to me on a unicorn or trailing pixie dust.

Some would have ulterior motives, like the woman a former colleague of mine met after he became a widower.

He believed she was the new love of his life and married her. Then, only three months after their vows, he lost his house to the caviar chaser.

Some other of my acquaintances shared eerily similar cautionary tales.

When it came to Vivian and me, we agreed a prenup was a way to protect each other and what we were building together. We started our life together as equals.

Looking back at my long dating odyssey, I'm relieved my willpower held up.

At times, it seemed my story would end with me plopped on a La-Z-Boy, telling stories to kids in exchange for them finding my misplaced TV remote.

Oscar Wilde once said "experience is simply the name we give our mistakes." Well, in that case, I'm now a sage!

My biggest blunder was treating dating like a video game. When things glitched with someone, I didn't troubleshoot. I just hit "new game," swiped on someone else, and hoped for a better score.

My former addiction to Sid Meier's *Civilization* video game had nothing on dating apps. The same itch was there—the need to check progress and claim new territory.

Every lull in the day became a chance to see who responded, or if some new nation, er, rather, woman had appeared on my "game" map.

Even my iPhone noticed. When I checked the total on-screen time on dating apps, it was close to three hours a day.

I was in a serious relationship—with my phone.

Determined to reel in my addiction, I limited my dating app time to twenty minutes over morning coffee and another twenty over a glass of wine after work.

A side benefit was that rather than

typing out a hurried message between phone calls at work, I had the focus and time to say what I meant, instead of firing off words I later regretted. Spending less time on the apps made time management critical.

If a conversation started feeling shallow or stuck, I'd simply say, "I've enjoyed chatting, but I think our conversation has run its course. Take care, and good luck with your search!"

Take, for example, the woman I had been chatting with for three weeks. She was pretty, educated, and funny, *but* still hadn't agreed to meet.

I came to realize I was her side guy, a man to joke and chat with, but nothing more. We parted.

When I first started online dating, I responded to every "hi" out of politeness. But if there was no spark, it was a mutual waste of time, like the time a fifty-year-old widow tried to snag a date by trash talking my faith.

"Why does your profile say you're Christian but you'll date someone who's not? That's weird."

From her tone, you'd think dating outside my faith put me in danger of getting turned into a pillar of pudding.

Trying to lighten it up a bit, I told her, "Faith matters, but I'm not checking baptism certificates at the door. I'm flexible if someone can accept me for who I am."

"THEN YOU'RE NOT A CHRISTIAN!"

Wow, I thought. *What is this—Monty Python's Spanish Inquisition?"*

In the spirit of that classic BBC TV show, I "changed the channel" to another potential date, and counseled myself for starting a conversation with her in the first place.

Prior to my decision to limit my online dating time, I'd spend hours on line debating politics with strangers.

Sometimes I felt like a steak being grilled from the right side, then seared with intense heat from the left.

Within days of each other, a hard-core Republican and a devoted Democrat both flamed me for refusing to hate the opposite party.

It started with a divorcee from Riverside who chatted with me on the phone, drilling down to find out if I supported Trump.

"I'm a registered independent," I said. "Honestly, I'm not a fan of either party right now. Our nation needs to find its way back to the middle."

"Yeah, but do you like Trump? If so, we're done."

That was something we could agree on. Goodbye.

Then, a few days later, a blackjack dealer from Pechanga Resort Casino asked me over the phone if I was a radical lefty.

Man. I thought. *What happened to small talk?*

When I mentioned my disillusionment with polarized politics, I heard dead silence from the other end.

In my mind, she was visualizing me with a barbed tail and horns. Our first call was our last.

What I came to realize is that when it came to politics and religion, I didn't require a partner who mirrored my views.

I needed someone with patience and tolerance for others—and the grace to listen. In return, I promised the same.

Sometimes the online dating drama became too much. I took a detox, pausing my accounts.

Instead, I'd chill with Sangria, watch *The Simpsons*, or do the Happy Baby yoga pose. The stiffness in my index finger from excessive swiping began to fade.

I wasn't giving up, just plugging myself back into life "outside the phone."

Relying *only* on dating apps became a stress of its own.

When I wasn't getting messages or likes I internalized that as I wasn't likeable enough. I countered that by simultaneously meeting new people face-to-face.

I'd go out on dates arranged by friends, start a conversation in the produce section of Aldi, or walk over to greet folks having coffee outside my church.

My quest to find new love took six years.

The majority of the thirty-some single women I met turned out to be once-and-done speed dates. No sparks flew.

It was more like a case of mild static cling.

In some cases, I remember some of their profile handles better than their real names. Who could forget Better Date Than Never and Profiles Encouraged?

What worked for me was posting my profile simultaneously on Zoosk, Match, and Plenty of Fish.

Rather than choose a niche site like "Buxom Shieldmaidens who Love Canasta," or "Old Farts Seeking Young Women," I chose popular apps with options for everyone that wouldn't cost more than my Social Security check, or a gold coin.

Vivian and I found each other on Plenty of Fish, but I met wonderful people on Zoosk and Match as well.

Learning how to best navigate the wilds of online dating apps wasn't just a simple "read the manual and go for it" kind of mission.

Embracing "match madness," I morphed into a human sponge—soaking up advice from anyone who swiped.

One tip I learned was to carefully read a profile, Google their name, *then* contact them.

Vivian Googled me before she agreed to meet. I don't blame her. "George Smith" sounds made up.

Fortunately, my name popped into her search engine for articles I'd written. One even had a photo of me when I was an Army DJ.

Before we met, she knew things about me that I'd forgotten.

Another great idea a date shared with me was to put *my* name into the search engine to make sure no one had channeled their Photoshop skills to post photos of me creating naked snow angels with woodland creatures. (That was in the days before AI!)

After days honing my profile with witty words, my biggest disappointment was that *virtually no one read it!*

Message after message confirmed it.

"Do you like tattoos?" asked one blonde who had exchanged messages with me, then gave me her phone number. (My profile said I didn't.)

"I'm old-fashioned when it comes to ink," I said. "I'm not much of a fan."

"You said you were in the Army, right?" she continued. Then she described her "tat," as "an American flag that stretched from hip to shining hip" on her back.

It sounded to me like a jumbo tramp stamp.

When I started stammering and stuttering, she interjected, "What's with you? Aren't you patriotic?"

Another woman, Sue, a petite brunette who worked for the city of Temecula, sent me a message saying she was interested.

Flattered, I was certain it was my witty bio and world travel experience that grabbed her attention.

When I gave her a follow-up call, I found I was wrong. It was the photos.

"Nice hiking shot," she said. "I recognize where you were. The Santa Rosa Plateau, right?"

After complimenting her on picking that out, we started comparing my federal government job and her city government job.

"Do they make you walk twenty-five feet from the building to smoke?" asked Sue. "My boss does. We even have to do it in the rain! She has no consideration for people!"

"You smoke?" I asked. (I'd made it clear in my bio that puffers were a "no-go" for me.)

"Yeah," she said. "But not much. I'm a social smoker."

"I've heard that before," I said, thinking back to the only smoker I'd dated before, when I was in my twenties.

"Social smoker. Isn't that like saying you're a little bit pregnant?"

"Well," she said. "What I mean by that is a smoke here and there at work, one or two at a bar, and another after sex. I always enjoy one then."

Then she laughed.

"Sue," I replied, "I'm guessing you didn't read my bio. I'm not a fan of smoking."

Silence.

Finally, she said, "Oh. You're one of those." *Click.*

Yup. She hung up on me.

Time after time, I'd go out on dates and fish for compliments on my writing and humor, only to get glassy eyes and "huh?"

My experience proved that when it comes to online dating, the three most important things are: photos, photos, and—photos.

Ironically, though, a profile with *just* pictures is a red flag as well.

People who take the time to fill in a bio show they're serious—even though prospective dates don't usually read the words. They just notice the white space!

What photos worked for me?

A quality head-and-shoulders shot, a full body photo, and a snapshot of me hiking to show I had a functional cardiovascular system—and didn't wilt in direct sunlight.

The profiles I most often clicked on had the same formula of a close-up, full body, and activity shot.

Since I was looking for a new love—not a "get a girlfriend *and* a dog, cat, or child thrown in for free" deal—I passed on someone whose main profile picture was of a woman snuggling with her dog, smiling with her children, or babysitting the grandkids.

Once, I saw a profile featuring a woman

257

hugging a toy prince. I booed out loud, threw a dinner roll at my screen, and kept swiping.

As for me, I focused on presenting the best version of myself.

I had a nip and tuck and used Just for Men hair dye. Instead of letting my ears and nose sprout "tumbleweeds," I had them waxed.

But still, I never lied about my age. My profile included a recent head-and-shoulders photo along with the accurate number of times I orbited the sun.

While self-deprecating humor is my default mode, I resisted writing a profile that said I was "on extended warranty," or a "vintage man."

Calling attention to my age was like highlighting the rust on a classic car and expecting applause.

Being honest with myself was critical. It was in one of these moments of introspection that I leveled with myself.

One weakness I had was that pretty faces lured me in like a siren calling out to a sailor. Entranced, I made stupid mistakes and missed red flags.

I freshened my profile with up-to-date photos and even tried a few different usernames—so someone who'd passed before might give me a second chance.

Rather than falling back on the cliche "guy with a sense of humor seeks the same," I sprinkled in quips so prospects could draw their own conclusion that I was (hopefully) an entertaining fella.

Before searching for someone new, I improved the "product" I was advertising: me.

I pride myself on staying calm and positive— sprinkling a little levity on life's garbage. But no amount of sparkle can make a bad situation smell like lilies.

Positivity and politeness have their place, but some situations call for instant, honest, direct communication.

I adjusted my approach, starting with humor to try and diffuse a difficult situation, *but then* transitioned into actively listening to the other person to discover what was wrong so we could fix it.

Another key was for me to be serious about myself. A "come to George" chat was awkward, but necessary.

George Inner Voice One: "*George, you may consider yourself a work of art, but Rubenesque is out now—especially for men.*"
George Inner Voice Two: "*Huh?*"

While I was in denial, it was true. My dad bod needed chiseling.

My abs were shy, hiding under a protective layer of blubber. Rather than blame Papa Time, I traded biscuits for biceps by reducing the carbs and working out more.

My goal wasn't to transform into the

Pale Hulk. I just wanted to bend down without my joints sounding like they were rubbing together hard enough to spark a fire.

I changed my walk route from the couch to the fridge to walking a mile from the house and back, then started yoga and weight lifting.

Instead of binging on peanut butter milkshakes, pizza, pasta, and burgers, I introduced seldom-seen substances to my intestines: leafy green vegetables and omega-3-rich fish.

The result? I became about fifteen pounds less of a man.

Investing in me, I plopped down cash for a lower facelift to eradicate my turkey neck. Next, I relocated part of my body north, filling in the bags under my eyes with 100 percent pure George belly fat.

My clothing needed to match my new "bod." I wore my pants and shirts until they frayed, then concealed them beneath a pile of secondhand DVDs—camouflage so Goodwill would accept them.

A well-meaning female friend of mine once told me even my *new* clothes shouted "old."

"Why do you tuck your T-shirt into your pants? To show off that your belt matches your leather shoes? That's something my grandpa does!"

It took me until my sixties to correct that faux pas and others.

When I learned that one of the first things women notice about a man is his shoes, I knew I was in trouble.

If my loafers could talk, they'd say, "Style for this guy is whatever his ex-wife didn't throw out!"

Once, I went on a date to a nice restaurant overlooking the California beach with black leather loafers and a tucked-in shirt. The host, a slender blonde who appeared to be in her twenties, glanced down at my footwear, working hard to conceal a smile. She wore sneakers.

Well, it took me decades, but I've finally achieved shoe nirvana—a pair for every occasion.

When I first started dating, changing my mindset from "married" to single was like trying to rewire my house blindfolded.

I struggled with emotions while juggling work, raising a teenage daughter, and supporting a son working on his degree.

Self-absorbed, I misread my kids' feelings. After Vivian and I exchanged vows, I held long talks with my kids about those difficult times.

"The break-up shocked us," said Brandon. "Why didn't you tell us what was coming?"

"We argued privately," I told him. "My parents fought in front of me, and I didn't want to repeat the mistake. It made me feel miserable."

Following up, I asked him what he thought of our situation in 2025.

"Yes, I wish we were still one family, but now I'm happy for you both," he said. "But it does make it hard to celebrate together for holidays."

Shannon shattered my mistaken notion that I was plugged into her feelings since we lived in the same house.

"Dad, I sat in my room crying because I missed my friends. I was hurting too."

My girl said she didn't want to worry me with her problems.

While I was dating, Shannon felt I was focusing more on the way a woman looked and her age, rather than her other attributes.

She hoped that once *she* got older, her husband would value her intelligence and personality, not just her appearance.

"Baby, trips around the sun had nothing to do with why your mom and I divorced. It's just over time we grew apart, and what we wanted from life changed. For me, the final split came when she refused to give life in the States a chance."

Fortunately, my birth kids and stepdaughter supported my new marriage. What came as a surprise to me, my former wife, Brigitte did as well.

Brigitte walked up to Vivian and chatted at a party celebrating Shannon's college graduation.

"George is a nice guy," she said, balancing a paper plate stacked high with tacos and pointing at me.

Of course, I would have preferred something less generic than "nice." Something along the lines of:

"He's smarter than Musk and funnier than Chappelle. The California sun baked my brain. We never should have gotten divorced."

On my son's birthday, my ex and current wife joined Brandon, Shannon, and me for a one-day hike.

At one point, Brigitte and Vivian trailed us. I pulled my son aside, whispering about my concerns that the two of them were comparing notes.

"I'm worried, son. I've never told Vivian about the gold bullion I stashed in Switzerland, my ten Bitcoins, or the sack of rubies I left in a safety deposit box in the Cayman Islands."

Brandon chuckled, saying I should chill.

Taking his advice, I cocked my head, aiming my ears in their direction, but all I heard was water flowing and birds chirping.

Twice, when I glanced back, Brigitte extended her hand to steady my wife as she gingerly stepped on rocks to cross a stream.

Another time, she shed her jacket and handed it to my wife to wear.

Walking over to my former wife, I thanked her for ensuring Vivian didn't fall in.

Vivian and Brigitte achieved something rare for a current and former wife: liking each other. It made the day enjoyable for all.

It would have been impossible for me to trudge through my online odyssey without the support of my "mini me's."

Brandon and Shannon grounded, advised, and loved me on a journey littered with endless cups of lattes and long car trips.

When I divorced, I was sixty-two. When Vivian and I exchanged vows in "Thee Olde Wedding Chapel," I was sixty-eight.

Hey, I told myself later when I took time to think. *If a pushing seventy-year-old average-looking dude with arthritic knees can find love, there's hope for everyone!*

Throughout my late-inning love search, faith in myself and patience kept me going. When that waned, I talked with my sprouts.

"Dad," said Shannon. "Don't worry. You're funny, loving, and handsome!"

"Jane's treating you like a patient, not a boyfriend. Dad, you can do better," said Brandon.

When I embarked on my odyssey, I thought having my teenage daughter in the house would have made dating awkward at best, impossible at the worst.

Yes, it was uncomfortable at times. But we made it work.

What helped me in my relationship with Vivian is that I never had to guess what she felt.

After we were married, she told me that I didn't "wow" her on the first date. But I was the fella who kept on showing up every day until she never wanted me to leave.

What she meant by that was it's hard for a sixty-something-year-old man to make a spectacular first impression on a woman on looks alone. But, in her case, the more she came to know me, the more she came to know I was a really swell fella.

Okay, that's me paraphrasing. I don't want to get mushy.

Yup. There I go again, joking about sentimental matters. Some of the women I dated said I should dial back the one-liners, cut back the sarcasm, or, at the very least, grow up.

Vivian, on the other hand, recognized that laughter is a central part of who I am, and accepted it.

When it comes to *her* sense of humor, my wife has one, but it's not a Robin Williams-like machinegun of quips. She's more like Claire in *Modern Family*, or Elaine in *Seinfeld*.

I love that quality about her. When I throw some tongue-in-cheek words her way and she takes them seriously, it makes the moment twice as funny.

Not only can the lady take a joke, she rolls with it, and amplifies it. At our wedding, our ordained-from-the-internet minister noted she was wearing the "biggest rock in Southern

California."

Vivian turned with a huge smile to family and friends and showed it off—a plastic two-inch ring with a flashing light!

While Vivian and my views on politics and religion sometimes differed, we listened to each other, embraced what we had in common, and sometimes agreed to disagree.

Our mutual passion to travel has already yielded great stories.

We started with smaller trips jetting from California to Pennsylvania to meet my mom and siblings. We drove our rental car up to the farmhouse in the Amish part of the state at one in the morning.

My sister, Lorri, left a light on for us as we unpacked under the moon and stars, hearing nothing but a chorus of frogs and crickets from the ponds.

The next morning, as I brushed my teeth in the downstairs bathroom, I heard a scratch, scratch, followed by our bedroom door opening, then a startled yell—and laugh.

My sister's golden retriever, Mack, had opened the door and jumped into bed with Vivian. The family's other pooch, Elliot, whom they called a "Puerto Rican street dog," jumped in too.

"As soon as I heard her laughing when the dogs jumped up, I knew she was a keeper," said Lorri.

After that, we both started visiting

countries on our bucket list—the island of Tahiti and New Zealand for me, Japan and Germany for her.

Vivian amazed me with her energy and zest to try challenges in her mid-fifties. She learned how to surf in Costa Rica and showed deadeye "Annie Oakley" skills on a pistol range in Pennsylvania.

We lived through challenges to laugh about them later.

In Thailand, I was giving her a massage in a pitch black room when Vivian unexpectedly jerked up and slammed her nose into my skull so hard it unleashed a crimson waterfall. I thought I broke it, but ice and elevation stopped it.

Gone was our plan to go diving in the crystal-blue waters off the Phi Phi islands.

While my Moderna COVID-19 vaccine and boosters had shielded me from the bug, it finally caught up with me on our cruise to Alaska.

Right after enjoying the sight of chunks of blue glacier ice sloughing off into the ocean with a distant rumble and huge splash, my nose turned into a spigot I couldn't turn off. Other than feeling a bit more tired than usual, that was my only symptom.

While I'm a giver, I didn't want to share with Vivian, but I did.

When we got home to California, it hit her like a frontal charge from the four horses of the Apocalypse: Fever, Headache, Runny nose, and Breathing.

Her doctor prescribed Paxlovid, and she recovered in a day.

In Japan, after a day of walking twelve miles, followed by a second day of walking ten, my creaky arthritic knees and bowlegs shouted, "Stop listening to your brain. It's in denial. You're old!"

To make it to the Meiji Shrine, I had to pop painkillers like they were Skittles.

Despite those occasional aches and pains over the next three years, we made it to France, Spain, Portugal, England and many more countries.

Sure, we had disagreements on our trips, but we overcame them with compromise.

Take Barcelona, for example.

Me—the guy with a no-go in land navigation back in the Army—decided I should be the one to guide us through the city with Google Maps.

The problem? I kept pocketing my phone because I'd seen lots of YouTube videos on thieves snatching them from the outstretched hands of tourists.

When I mistakenly took us fifteen minutes in the wrong direction, Vivian turned frostier than a tray of ice cubes.

Our solution? I pocketed my phone, my wife fished out hers and she did the rest of the navigation.

Demoted to sentry duty, I watched for suspicious cyclists plotting "snatch-and-pedals."

Another key to our relationship is, as Vivian wisely said (and I agree): "Be picky before you marry, but once you do, focus only on your partner's good qualities and let the rest slide."

Whew! Screening passed!

Looking back, I'm happy love didn't retire when I divorced in my sixties.

I didn't start a seniors' e-bike gang or putter through the neighborhood in a golf cart enforcing HOA rules.

Instead, the gray wolf with a limp wandered into the wilds of online dating—where the odds were stacked against him—and somehow came out with a happily-ever-after.

It turned out all those cautionary tales were just fairy tales.

Red Riding Hood fell for him, and they got married. Even grandmother would've approved if she were still alive, but she died of old age long before they met.

Now, the gray wolf is "swiped out."

P.S. Thanks to yoga, lifting, and walking, his joints are holding up just fine.

The Lumbar Gallery

A face for radio—my dating profile picture in 2016.

When I divorced in 2016, I was working at a perfect job for a guy who loves to talk: the worldwide spokesman for the American Forces Network (AFN). But balancing job, daughter, and dating was as easy as juggling machetes.

After my divorce, daughter Shannon *(top, far right)*
invited friends from Germany to join her friends
from the States. I made chow for six kids.

For one summer after my divorce, I was "one of the girls," showing three of Shannon's German friends as many California beaches as I could fit into one month.

In late 2016, a truck turned my Honda Fit into a pancake. Somehow I avoided becoming syrup.

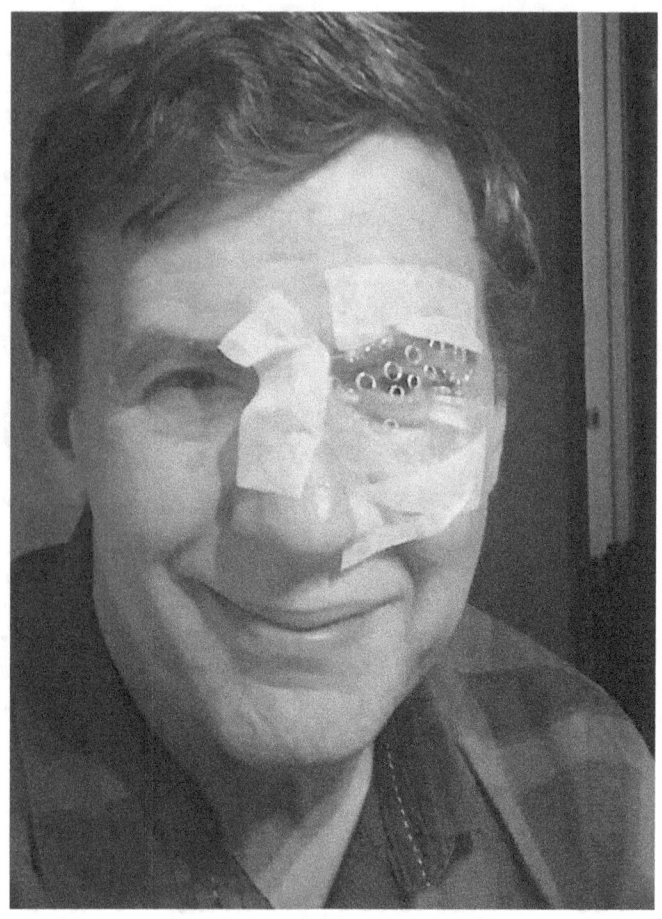

When I needed cataract surgery, looking to better
myself, I asked if there was such a thing as a pair of
"introspective lenses."

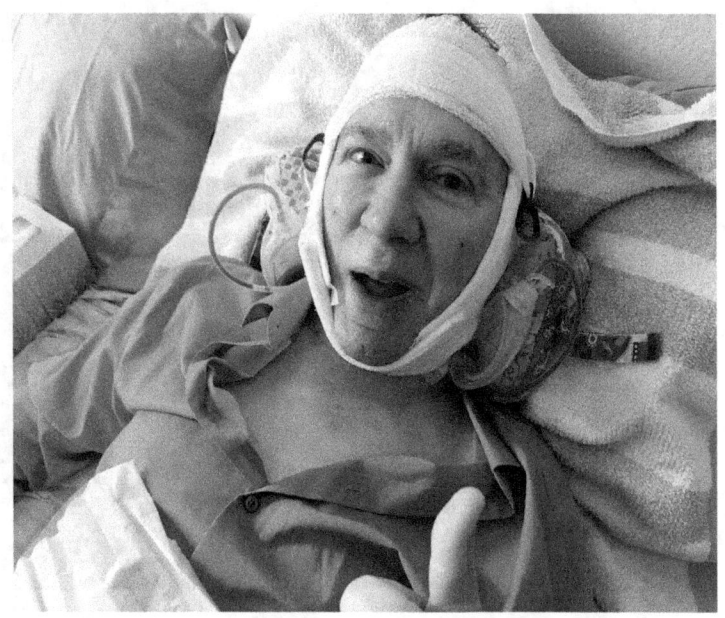

In 2019, a girlfriend said nip and tuck would fix my gobbler neck. After I got it, she said I needed plastic surgery to fix my plastic surgery.

In January 2020, my daughter Shannon and I went to Tijuana to build up our immunity against the coronavirus with Coronas—and Margaritas.

Here I am with Shannon, Idalia, and Brandon
during the pandemic. I'm lucky I made it to another
birthday celebration. My filter mask is only
covering one nostril.

A profile in courage. Me without a mask,
celebrating my birthday. That's my son Brandon,
with his face squished against the door
window—*thinking* "happy birthday to you."

My babe magnet—a rental built in the 1950s.

While I lost confidence in myself after my divorce,
my kids were always next to me, or over my
shoulder— sometimes, literally.

Vivian proudly holds up the largest rock in California—a two-inch-plastic ring that lit up. The minister is the internet-ordained "Reverend" Larry Sichter.

Our love of travel took us to this yoga studio in
Costa Rica. P.S. Bet you're glad I'm not flashing *my*
bare belly.

Vivian's shirt sums it up.

Thanks for reading *Love, Lies & Lumbar Pain!*

Please consider leaving an honest review online. Authors like me rely on readers like you to get the word out on our books!

George A. Smith

Acknowledgements

Thanks to my son Brandon for enhancing my life. He was four, and on my shoulders, when I whacked his head into a low castle beam. In minutes he morphed into a unicorn.

I'm grateful he now seems relatively normal and correctly recalls his name two out of three times.

Props to daughter Shannon for spicing up my life and my book.

As a miniature human, she jumped barefoot on a trampoline in the snow in Germany, waded through the frigid waters of the North Sea in January, and frolicked outside in a forest kindergarten.

Today, she continues her rugged outdoor life with bare feet resembling old penny loafers.

A special thanks to my lovely, intelligent wife and master baker Vivian for giving me a pass on the honey-do list while I was writing this book.

Stepdaughter Allie, deserves credit too. She puts up with my shenanigans and even admits she knows me when we go out in public.

Props to my editors: Lucile Harrington, Maggie Esterrios, Jef Reilly, Jo Bordeau, Renita Menyhert, and Michelle Drumheller.

Finally, thank you to Get Covers for collaborating with me, putting up with my many changes, and designing a catchy book cover.

The Author's First Misadventures

Soldier of the Airwaves: Defending Democracy One Song at a Time. A teenager from Amish country enlists as an Army DJ during the Vietnam War, beginning a life of adventure and a storied career spanning decades and continents.

George A. Smith: "When I opened my mic in the 1970s at U-Tapao, Thailand, I played music and cracked jokes, unaware people tuned in for more than entertainment. In 1973, troops dialed in for breaking news on the planes crashing around them in rice paddies.

As the Cold War raged in Europe, my fellow American DJs and I introduced a continent to wild, unpredictable music.

After dodging bullets, mortars, and improvised explosive devices in Iraq and Afghanistan, U.S. warriors returned to base and decompressed with my network's live TV sports.

Join me for behind-the-mic stories filled with humor, history, and home. Learn about how America's GI broadcasters influenced hall of fame rockers, shaped the attitudes of foreign politicians, and championed freedom of speech."

Enjoy chapters like "From Amish Buggies to Thai Weed," "Complaints from a Heavily Armed Audience," "The Assassination and Me," and "Backstage: Late Night With David Letterman."

The foreword is by a former Commanding General of the U.S. Army Europe, Lt. Gen.

(retired) Mark Hertling, who went on to become a military news analyst for cable news outlets.

He said, "I loved reading this book, because George's life was my life. His stories are jaw droppingly cool . . . and the fun he had made me smile."

The book is available in paperback, hardcover, e-book, and audiobook at Amazon and other bookstores.

It's also on display at the National Capital Radio & Television Museum in Bowie, Maryland.

www.ingramcontent.com/pod-product-compliance
Lightning Source LLC
Chambersburg PA
CBHW060412130626
46555CB00005B/2038